Tangerine Dream

in the 1970s

Stephen Palmer

SONICBOND

sonicbondpublishing.com

Sonicbond Publishing Limited
www.sonicbondpublishing.co.uk
Email: info@sonicbondpublishing.co.uk

First Published in the United Kingdom 2021
First Published in the United States 2021

British Library Cataloguing in Publication Data:
A Catalogue record for this book is available from the British Library

ISBN 978-1-78952-161-0

Typeset in ITC Garamond & ITC Avant Garde
Printed and bound in England

Graphic design and typesetting: Full Moon Media

DECADES

Tangerine Dream

in the 1970s

Stephen Palmer

SONICBOND

sonicbondpublishing.com

Acknowledgements

Thanks to Peter Beasley, Dave Bessell, Stephen Bradbury, Dave Buxton, Jez Creek, Michael Daniel, Neil Jellis, Steve Jones, Jerry Kranitz, Cyndee Lee Rule, Howard Scarr and Alan Walker.

Special Thanks to Wouter Bessels, Andy King and Stephen Lambe.

Very Special Thanks to Steve Dinsdale, David Elliott, Steve Jolliffe and Steve Schroyder.

This book is dedicated to the memory of Edgar Froese.

DECADES | Tangerine Dream in the 1970s

Contents

Introduction – Berlin, Art, Music

Edgar Froese had a musical problem. He wanted to create a new European music, but all he heard around him were American groups and artists. That American sound and its British equivalent were everywhere in 1967: on the radio, on 45 rpm vinyl singles, on the 33 rpm album format. What should he do?

Born on 6 June 1944 in Tilsit, East Prussia (now Russia), Froese's family was devastated by World War II, his father and some other family members killed by the Nazis during the conflict. With his mother and other family survivors, he moved to Berlin. In the mid-1950s he took up the piano, then a few years later the guitar. However, it was art that motivated him more than anything, and after enrolling in the Berlin Academy of the Arts he studied sculpture and painting. In a 2010 interview with *The Quietus*, he said, 'I used to work on big canvas formats and had several exhibitions, even during my time being a student at art school. But finally, the music became a stronger focus point ... Even today I still try to express myself by painting a lot and working on computer graphics'.

But art and music were not the only interests for his active mind. Undertaking a degree in the evenings, he also studied philosophy and psychology, receiving a doctorate for his submission on Immanuel Kant's categorical imperative: a method of evaluating motivations for action.

From a young age, Froese felt part of something larger than just nationality. In his interview with *The Quietus* he said, 'People my age have grown up with all the post-war memories – privations on all levels of a daily life ... I personally never felt I was part of a specific nationality. I was a so-called cosmopolitical person from day one'.

Music, though, continued to attract him. In 1965 he formed an R&B band – The Ones – who a short time later became part of the burgeoning psychedelic scene. A single – 'Lady Greengrass' on Star-Club Records – was their only public document. (Froese later dismissed this phase of his musical career in an interview with David Elliott's trailblazing *Neumusik* fanzine, by saying The Ones were a band of shitty idiots: absolute amateurs.) However, this musical odyssey led him in due course to gig dates in Spain, where one day The Ones were invited to play at Salvador Dali's villa in Cadaqués. Froese told *The Quietus*:

> Dali was quite a big influence in my life because his philosophy of being as original and authentic as possible had touched me very intensively

> at that time ... I invested a lot of time ... training myself to follow such a philosophical path. When I met Dali the first time, I was 22 – a youngster who knew immediately that nearly everything is possible in art as long as you have a strong belief in what you're doing.

This encounter with the surrealist icon turned out to be a milestone in Froese's life. In an interview given to issue 14 of *Prog Magazine,* he recalled those times:

> During one of our longer conversations in his olive garden in Cadaqués, Dali was saying that he decided to be against everything the public like and adore. So if the masses like democracy, he stands for dictatorship and the other way 'round. 'If you're a divine individual, you have to think and behave outside every rule the bourgeoisie tries to dictate', he explained ... As an artist and cosmopolitan being, he was absolutely fascinating. On August 8th 1967, we performed *The Resurrection of Rotten Christianity – Music for a Sculpture*. It took place at a happening ... behind his home and atelier, in front of a sculpture built out of Coca-Cola cans, some flotsam he found in the sea and olive tree branches.

Dali's near-fanatical method of working, and his intellectual stance, encouraged Froese to follow a more experimental musical path. So in 1967, with The Ones no longer active, he created a new musical vehicle. As he told *Prog* magazine, he wanted to 'do the same thing as (Dali) did in painting, in music'. This new vehicle had a distinctive name: Tangerine Dream.

It was autumn in the year of peace and love. By now, Froese had met and recruited a number of musicians for his new group: drummer Lanse Hapshash, bassist Kurt Herkenburg, vocalist Charly Prince and multi-instrumentalist Volker Hombach. By 1968 this lineup had performed a concert at Berlin's Technical University – their music much influenced by the wave of free, psychedelic rock sweeping the world. Froese played guitar – loud and wild. By the end of 1968, the band had played a gig at Germany's largest festival, the Internationalen Essener Songtage, having acquired an enthusiastic underground following.

Not everything was working out, however. With drummer Hapshash departing to be replaced by Sven-Åke Johansson, the end was in sight, and by spring 1969 the band's opening phase was over.

A fragment of film footage exists from these very early days. Titled 'Sing This All Together', and broadcast on the television documentary 'Deutschland Erwacht – Popmusic Aus Deutschen Landen' on 26 September 1968, it shows a youthful Froese with a hint of a beard, playing guitar alongside a violinist and a singer. The accompanying music freaks out in Floydian style.

During these two years, Froese and his cohorts played many gigs at Berlin's Zodiak Arts Lab, a venue founded by Hans-Joachim Roedelius and Conrad Schnitzler. Froese still felt the pull of music, art and the underground scene, so not too long after disbanding Tangerine Dream he reformed the group, playing over the next few months with a variety of musicians, including Steve Jolliffe, who in later years would make quite an impact on the group's music. Froese even worked briefly with Nik Turner – soon to become sax and flute main man for counterculture titans Hawkwind.

In an interview exclusive to this book, I asked Steve Jolliffe about those early days:

SP: You were at the Berlin Konservatorium in 1969. How did you encounter the Tangerine Dream of those formative years?

SJ: I met Edgar in a Berlin studio which I had gone to visit. I heard they were producing some electronic music. I was studying composition and piano and had always been fascinated by the development of electronic music. Edgar was at a crossroads and was wondering what his next move should be. I suggested forming a three-piece and create purely improvised experimental music. He was a bit perturbed at the loss of a band concept, with no bass player, but he was always willing to try something new, so we started looking for a drummer, and finally settled on a tall skinny kid by the name of Klaus Schulze.

SP: Playing with the group in local places at that time, must have been interesting. What kind of music were you all making?

SJ: We played many gigs throughout Germany and Holland, mostly in small *avant-garde* type clubs. I loved it, but I needed a break from Germany and decided to return to England – our last gig was in Wiesbaden. We lost most of our equipment off the roof rack of the car. So I went home penniless and instrumentless. Edgar called me a few months later saying he had managed to secure a record deal, and would I like to come back. But I decided to join a band in London.

SP: What was your approach to improvisation?

SJ: I have always been an improviser, after an early incident at a gig where the band wanted me to play a set-piece. It was a disaster and put me off ever copying other people's work for the rest of my life.
SP: How did your approach compare with Edgar Froese's?
SJ: I love being close to the source when I create music, often keeping first takes and doing my best to switch off the internal dialogue – throwing aside any preconceptions. I think Edgar had a similar attitude. A lot of his riffs seem to be influenced by the blues, and he was a big fan of Pink Floyd. We went to see them once in a school hall in London: there were only about fifty people there.

For Froese, however, the lineup was still not right. He broke up the group, only to reform it once again, this time with his friend Conrad Schnitzler from the Zodiak Arts Lab. It was autumn 1969, and Schnitzler shared Froese's interest in creating experimental music. But there was one other factor in this new version of the band. One of the regulars of the Zodiak scene was a youthful, energetic, but sensitive drummer by the name of Klaus Schulze. With him and Schnitzler, Froese would at last create a band lineup strong and vital enough to gain record company interest. His path was set. Though he did not know it, the future beckoned.

Even though these were formative days, film footage does exist of Froese, Schulze and one 'Happy Dieter' (the man never revealed his surname according to Schulze and soon-to-be manager Klaus D. Müller) on bass: a seven-minute fragment known as *The Bath Tube Session*. Filmed at the St. George Fountain in the courtyard of a restaurant on Potsdamer Strasse in 1969, this extraordinary footage shows Froese already with his distinctive long hair, moustache and trimmed-beard combo. The music is wild and improvised. Froese appears cool, even a little remote, whereas 'Happy Dieter' grooves comfortably on bass, while Schulze – unsurprisingly – beats the hell out of his drum kit, resplendent in waistcoat and love beads.

In an interview at *klaus-schulze.com,* Schulze remarked:

Drumming was very important. Although I was very tired of the sound of a drum set in the early seventies, and did not use any drums for my first albums, I only realized later that the perfect rhythm is very important ... I learned a lot about a 'perfect rhythm' from Michael Shrieve, (who) a few years later ... visited me in my studios, stayed for a while and taught me some essential things about rhythm. These were things that I didn't

> know, even though I was more or less a professional drummer in the late sixties and early seventies. A rhythm should be like the heartbeat, like breathing. As Michael put it: 'You should be able to walk with the rhythm'.

The Bath Tube Session is a great piece of footage for all interested in the cultural stew in which Froese created the band.

Other early film fragments also exist – notably a minute or so of the Westdeutscher Rundfunk documentary *Krautrocker Essen Kein Sauerkraut*, which shows Froese and Thomas Kessler in the studio. Also present is the drummer Al Akhbar, and Steve Jolliffe playing flute, a saxophone slung around his neck. The band name Tangerine Dream is printed in suitably flowery lettering on Akhbar's kick drum. Subtitled 'Demonstration Within Limits (1969)', the clip intercuts Froese playing guitar with footage of demonstrations.

In Andy King's sleeve notes to the remastered 2012 Esoteric Recordings CD of *Electronic Meditation,* Schulze recalled:

> One day we played with Tangerine Dream at a festival in some castle. It lasted the entire weekend, and we visited Guru Guru, who lived somewhere around. And these guys dropped us some (LSD) trips into our tea. Just before the gig! Geez ... That was a gig! Conny Schnitzler had a violin with a pickup which he just held in front of the speaker, and it just screamed the whole time. Edgar told us later that he thought the guitar neck was ten meters long and he couldn't reach it. And me with my drums, I hit them and the sound arrived only half a minute later. Just for a brief moment, in one of those brighter moments you have on such trips, I saw a guy in the front row – he was ten meters away from me for sure, and I thought he stood right in front of me, and he just said, 'Man, these guys are kaputt'.

By now, though, Froese needed to commit some of the band's psychedelic music to tape. In October 1969, renting a factory in Berlin and acquiring a basic two-track Revox reel-to-reel machine, the trio of Froese, Schnitzler and Schulze recorded the music which the following year would be released on Ohr Records. Two other musicians – flautist Thomas Keyserling and keyboards man Jimmy Jackson – also played on the album, though they were uncredited in the original LP's sleeve notes.

Ohr Records was the brainchild of Rolf-Ulrich Kaiser, a German record producer and central figure on the Krautrock scene. The label released some of the earliest and most important Krautrock albums. Kaiser and Froese would go on to work together for four years, but in late 1969 the main thing on Froese's mind was a debut release for Tangerine Dream. Yet he and Kaiser first met by chance. Unknown to Froese, a tape of an early improvisation was passed to the Ohr supremo, who then wrote to Froese offering him a record contract and 1,000DM. Froese was surprised by this twist of fate, then greatly amused.

The end of the 1960s was nigh – 1970 lay just weeks away. What lay ahead for Froese was a debut release, and the beginning of one of the great musical journeys of the 1970s.

What then should he do with his musical life? Having realised that the solution to his problem of the glut of American music and American influences was to create a new European music, he applied himself with zeal to the task. He believed in what he was doing. He had tasted success and knew influential people. It was time to grasp the moment.

1970 – Music, Success, Ohr

As John Lennon said, the dream is over; but for Edgar Froese, the dream was just beginning. It was 1970, and he had interest from the Ohr record label.

The band were still playing concerts. In total, during this year, they played thirteen dates in Germany and one in Austria. But an album would allow them to give their fans something to listen to away from live concerts, and it would reinforce their status as a band of the moment with a future. An album release was essential.

Ohr had already released four early Krautrock LPs – by Floh de Cologne, Limbus 4, Bernd Witthüser and Embryo – a slew of albums all released during spring 1970. Number five on the list was to be the debut Tangerine Dream recording, set for June. Rolf-Ulrich Kaiser had heard the demo music recorded in the rented Berlin factory, and he was enthusiastic. His main stipulation was that the band accept the traditional Ohr cover design. The sleeve of *Electronic Meditation*, therefore, followed the Ohr design of the time. The first four Ohr LPs featured artwork by Reinhard Hippen, each one using dismembered baby doll parts as the imagery's main theme. *Electronic Meditation* had a stark white and magenta colour palette, its central image the back of a baby doll from which wires emerged, all set against what looks like a piece of protoboard.

Froese recalled the recording of the album in an interview given in January 1980 to David Elliott's *Neumusik* fanzine:

> In 1969, I met Klaus in Berlin. He was a very bad drummer, but he had some sort of craziness about him that I was looking for. That is what has happened with Tangerine Dream over the past ten years. All the people who went through the band, came into the band because they had some sort of craziness about them. That's what I think. It's the sort of music you can't create if you're absolutely normal ... *Electronic Meditation* was done by absolute amateurs. We couldn't handle our equipment, and during that period of recording, we couldn't get any record company interested in it. Rolf-Ulrich Kaiser was interested, and he gave us some money.

Schulze also recalled those early days in an interview given to Mark Prendergast, made available in the 1994 five-album Virgin Records box set *Tangents:*

> We recorded and toured *Electronic Meditation*. That, for me, is the primary electronic album. Edgar played guitar, Schnitzler organ and me drums through loads of effects. We were experimenting with a lot of random stuff and were making up our own sounds. I remember Conrad had this metal cup full of these bits of glass, in which he stuck a microphone attached to each machine. I played a lot of different percussive sounds that were then altered by machines. It was just great to be in a band who were open to so much experimentation.

Schulze, however, was not destined to remain with the band for long. Eight months after joining he departed, citing his wish to get married.

The gatefold LP was released with a cutout in which a stamped balloon resided. In Andy King's sleeve notes for the remastered 2012 Esoteric Recordings CD, Froese recalled:

> We did a lot of tape splicing and a lot of sound research as *we* understood it in those days. It was very exotic. Sounds were made using everyday objects – for example, a sieve filled with dry peas, an old office calculating machine (Conrad Schnitzler's addiator), two old iron bars and hard parchment paper, all recorded with a microphone and sent through reverbs and delays to create unusual sounds. The results could not always be used musically; it was all quite different from the commercial pop sound. Technically, the studio was very sparse. As we didn't have a lot of money, all the resulting sounds were directly mastered onto a Revox quarter-inch machine.

Electronic Meditation (1970)

Personnel:

Edgar Froese: guitars, organ, piano, sound effects, tapes, metal cup and broken glass

Klaus Schulze: drums, percussion, metal sticks, whip and burning parchment

Conrad Schnitzler: cello, violin, guitar, addiator

Jimmy Jackson: organ

Thomas Keyserling: flute

Recorded and produced in Berlin in October 1969 by Froese/Ulrich Weigel/Klaus Freudigmann

Release date: June 1970

Chart placings: -

Running time: 36:37

All tracks by Froese, Schulze, Schnitzler
Side One: 1. 'Genesis' 2. 'Journey Through A Burning Brain'
Side Two: 1. 'Cold Smoke' 2. 'Ashes To Ashes' 3. 'Resurrection'

Opening with deep-space noise in classic Pink Floyd style, the first cut's introduction features glissando guitar and organ drones alongside a few cymbal flourishes from Schulze. After a while Schnitzler's cello comes in playing shivery notes, before Keyserling's flute takes the lead – fast notes multiplying in high and low registers. As this solo line develops, Schulze turns his attention to the tom-toms, pounding out a fast rhythm against which the cello and organ drones fight. There is a lot going on now – sound in all directions, some of it indicating the formless void; some structured, notably the flute and drums. This is an interstellar jam session in overdrive, with the drums and splashy cymbals always propelling the piece forwards.

'Journey Through A Burning Brain' relies much more on psychedelic guitar tropes and a heavy rock vibe. Syd Barrett figures and licks are present at the beginning, but at its heart, Froese's playing here is surreal. The flute is a background instrument during the introduction, as heavy reverb swathes the music and the organ swirls this way and that. As the introduction concludes, a structured set of organ chords begins, with the surreal guitar lick still playing. Soon however that tiny bit of form fades, to be replaced with clonking noises and the repeating guitar lick, though the organ chords can still be heard. When they return, the mood is darker, with much made of the available organ whirring effects. Now the guitar transforms from repeated lick into semi-solo, individual plucked notes burnishing the music.

With the rise of a new organ variation, the music really heads off into space, reminiscent of Pink Floyd's *A Saucerful Of Secrets* in its choice of chords. Now a new backing begins – drums, guitars and a constant organ drone, ushering in the first proper psychedelic jam. Though this is Floydian territory, the musicians elaborate their sections with zeal and musicality. Froese is content to wring as many clashing notes, crashes and slides out of his instrument as possible, alternately reverberated and clean. Schulze meanwhile provides an impressionistic tom-based percussion carpet for the rest of the band to work with – cymbal work is minimal. As Froese's guitar backing goes into overdrive, he wrests a new sequence of notes out of his solo, developing a musical progression over which the high register flute sounds like birds escaping the flames – and with Froese pulling as many notes per second out of his instrument as he can, Schulze suddenly propels the music into intense, high energy rock: toms pounding, snare snapping and cymbals crashing everywhere. The track ends in organised chaos and the soothing tones of the organ returning... then the jam is over.

The ten minutes of 'Cold Smoke' are essentially a paean to inner space, opening with shimmering organ and deeply reverberated noises. Sudden explosions of guitar and drums punctuate the calm, however, indicating the possibility of mental danger. As weird clicking, buzzing and plunking sounds vibrate through the mix, a new vibe emerges: cautious, wary, watchful. This music is like the depiction of the aftermath of some terrible event, whose actuality is described by the organ/drum/guitar explosions. The listener never knows quite where they are.

In due course, a settled rhythm emerges, again propelled by Schulze and his pattering, rippling tom work. The guitar is an *avant-garde* show, supported by thin organ drones whose notes drift from one key to another. When Schulze's cymbals come in, the organ chords raise themselves into ever-higher registers; then, with downward glissandos, reset themselves.

After a while, the drums halt and the organ takes up a new theme; then we are off again into psychedelic jam territory, as Froese unleashes a distorted solo full of feedback. This solo is comparatively melodic, yet it also rips and tears through that squealing feedback via its flurry of psychedelic notes. Mixer effects (mostly reverb) augment the solo, adding to its hallucinatory quality as if the listener can never be certain from where it comes. Schulze, meanwhile, does everything he can to smash his drum kit into submission, adding yet another overwhelming, titanic performance to this album's roster. As the guitar solo comes to its climax, an extraordinary vocal accompaniment arrives, adding even more emotional angst to the jam. This voice is hard to comprehend, but its emotional tenor is obvious – anguished, wild, and delivered from some terrible emotional centre.

'Ashes To Ashes' is a more sedate jam, with the drums played in a much clearer recording, as is the electric guitar solo. There is energy and feeling, but none of the previous track's crazy primal chaos. Over all this, the flute plays a weird atonal part, as if unable to understand the music's vibe, yet willing to take part. Froese pulls out another flurry of notes as the music takes a more energetic turn, but this does not last long. Soon, the intensity diminishes, albeit underpinned by pounding drums.

The last cut, 'Resurrection', is at first an organ-dominated piece over which we hear a backwards voice – Froese reading the back of a ferry ticket – as if giving an account of an impossible venture. It is psychedelic to the max, taking advantage of every trope available. After just a minute or so, however, this section fades, to be replaced by a gliss-and-drone section augmented by cymbal strikes: the opening minutes of the album resurrected. It is 'Back to the start, the circle closes', as the LP sleeve notes explain. The listener is returned to space, having partaken of the terrestrial jam sessions. Free electronic rock is gone, and all that is left is the sparse drifting aftermath.

In an interview published in David Elliott's *Neumusik* fanzine, Chris Franke gave his reaction to this opening phase of the band he would join a year later:

> Yes, I think (*Electronic Meditation*) is maybe the best record in the form of spontaneous music or early progressive music. It is one example of one period of TD's music which was free from '68 to '71. It was an interesting period where music was influenced by progressive music, by free jazz, and by some *avant-garde* music. It was totally improvised (and very loud!) and was in some ways similar to today's new wave music. But it's very difficult to compare *Electronic Meditation* with records made in later periods, because it is in quite a different style, and if one likes this style of music, then it's not surprising that this album appeals the most.

Electronic Meditation was reviewed in music magazines of the time. The month after its release, it received mixed praise from a reviewer at the German *Sounds* magazine:

> ...an electronic rock excursion into a stereophonic nirvana. It is the kind of record that you love one evening, on the next, it bores you sick ... ('Cold Smoke' is) so fresh, lively and powerful as some of the things you like us to offer the serious concert of the so-called contemporary electronic music.

At the end of the year, the album was placed fifth in the *Sounds* annual readers' poll. It seemed, therefore, that Tangerine Dream had arrived. But where next?

1971 – Ohr, Kosmische, Concerts

Once more lacking a drummer for Tangerine Dream, Froese – performing routine studio work to make ends meet – found himself asked one day to replicate the guitar part of the Simon & Garfunkel song 'The Boxer' for a German version. It was through this chance request that he met a seventeen-year-old youth who happened to be a drummer. That young man would not only have a profound impact on Froese and Tangerine Dream, he would reroute the course of electronic music through the 1970s with his groundbreaking Moog work. His name was Christopher Franke.

Franke had something of a reputation as a drummer of various styles, including free jazz. Having studied with the Strasbourg Percussion Ensemble, he was particularly interested in the relationship between theatre and music. He was a member of Agitation Free (in which synth musician and later band guest Michael Hoenig also played), and was – conveniently for Froese – based in Berlin.

In Andy King's sleeve notes to the remastered 2012 Esoteric Recordings CD of *Electronic Meditation,* Franke recalled:

> Edgar and I understood each other very well from the beginning. He and I were very interested in working together because both of us wanted to get away from written music. We wanted to make long songs and improvise ... Edgar struck me as a serious thinker, into playing regular concerts. So we just improvised, and liked each other's ideas.
>
> At the time I met Edgar, my group Agitation Free was falling apart. He was in a transition at that time too. Tangerine Dream had fallen apart because Klaus Schulze and Conrad Schnitzler had just left the group ... Horizons opened for us – not only in classical and electronic, but also via East-Indian and African music. It was an eye-opener. When I decided to play with Edgar, I waved my education goodbye. From this time on, I must say, I worked as a professional musician. I was about seventeen, and my parents had to sign my first record contract. Edgar is nine years older than me, so that made some things interesting.

In the 1978 *Cyclone* tour programme, Franke recalled: 'They were making experiments with instruments, and also with visuals, pictures and exhibitions'.

The group performed concerts in Germany and Austria during 1971, and even managed a few television guest spots, including a concert for twelve pinball machines, cello, guitar and drums. This being live television, the nation was scandalised, and there followed much public protestation. On 19 June, the group performed at the Goethe University in Frankfurt; one week later playing at the Ossiach World Music Festival in Austria.

Schnitzler recalled those days of the trio in an interview with *Neumusik* in 1980:

> Sometimes we did fantastic things, but they were playing against me. Klaus Schulze didn't know anything about the music. I was older than him, and Edgar was in-between. I found it better with Franke than with Klaus, because Franke was very interested.

Up to now, Tangerine Dream had been an unstable lineup. But there was a further shock to come for Froese. He had asked Conrad Schnitzler to join the band (Schnitzler replying, 'You know I cannot play?') and had worked alongside all Schnitzler's *avant-garde* notions, but now Schnitzler was on the way out, leaving the band as Froese and the novice Franke. Yet Ohr was interested in releasing more music, and there were concerts to consider.

One of the best known of these concerts – of which a short filmed fragment exists – is the Ossiach Lake outdoor concert in Austria. In these images, Froese, with distinctive long blond hair, electric guitar in hand and facing an amplifier stack, sits in what appears to be a forest clearing beside the lake. The music is overdubbed at the beginning – featuring heavy use of gliss guitar and organs – but later on the music matches the hand movements of organist Peter Baumann, then a brand new recruit. Chris Franke, meanwhile, sitting on the ground in a manner most unbecoming for a drummer, crashes cymbals with a felt beater. The concert later spawned a triple LP titled Ossiach Live – recorded by ORF-Studio Klagenfurt – for which Tangerine Dream provided the eight-minute track 'Oszillator Planet Concert', which only saw the light of day on CD forty years later. The music drifts along to the thrum of organs, above and below which gliss guitars and heavy VCS3 sounds shimmer. It is very much in the manner of all their music of this formative period. Occasional bursts of more intense music contrast with psychedelic inserts – these not unlike some of Syd Barrett's slide guitar meanderings – which, against a thrumming, loping guitar riff, help conclude proceedings.

There was also television music. In 1971, German television showed a film called *Vampira*, to which Tangerine Dream provided the soundtrack.

Now publicly (non-commercially) available as just over 34 minutes of music, the soundtrack begins with much cosmic warbling of low register gliss guitars, before what sounds like early VCS3 noise filters coming in. This is a short introductory track.

The second, much longer track, is quieter and calmer, though the emphasis remains on gliss guitar. Drones and simple VCS3 whooshes can be heard in the background, with some of the drones sounding liked bowed electric guitar strings. There is also a ghostly organ sound, cosmic in tone, a sound which would be much used over the next two years. This spacey, ethereal track just floats for a few minutes, occasionally erupting into bursts of sound, then relaxing back into drone. Continuing, and always cosmic, occasional flutters of VCS3 emerge from the mix, always to return, along with some deeply reverberated guitar feedback swoops. Later on, there are what sound like theremin glissandos: classic horror film fare. At length, however, a new, deep organ chord enters the mix, and in a major key, giving a new impetus to the music, which then fades.

The third cut features the same spectral organ, but now with the addition of subtle cymbal crashes. VCS3 birdsong twitters in and out of the mix, but the emphasis is on the organ: playing a meandering theme to a single drone. After a while, a simple piano theme fades up, played to a continuous three-note ostinato. It has hints of jazz, though in tone and mood, it fits the ghostly atmosphere well. VCS3 drifts continue to spiral in and out of the mix. As the playing intensifies and gets more complex (it is not apparent who played this technically sophisticated part), the music intensifies to a sudden climax, then fades as the organ returns.

The fourth track is wonderfully ghostly, with eerie synth sirens matching percussive noises. As we hear a deep gliss guitar, a new, almost strident organ enters the mix, like the call of some church keyboard; then, just as suddenly, it fades, as does the music.

The fifth track opens with gunshots before another cosmic organ plays spectral chords – the timbre of this keyboard is reminiscent of Rick Wright. This sparse, tranquil music evokes deepest night, perhaps at the border of some swamp or forest border. As the organ deepens in tone, a whirring synth sounds, though the organ continues to dominate the music. A choir of gliss guitar sounds at length before the music fades.

The next track opens with whooshing white noise – presumably made by a VCS3 – before rolling guitar chords play a melancholy theme accompanied by a high register, bouncing keyboard part. After a while these two sounds are joined by VCS3 warbles and oscillations, which over the next few minutes intensify and transmute into what sounds like macabre speech. Then the track quietens as high-pitched VCS3 whines, then shrieks in a terrifically effective sound: synthesized screams.

The final cut also opens with tranquil, rippling organ chords before a curious, almost car-horn-like sound attracts the listener's attention. As the music rises in pitch, so does the sound, transmuting into a shimmering organ chord, which almost at once is joined by a hint of gliss guitar. These sounds are then fed into a rapid-time echo unit, as further new shimmering organ chords arrive. This music sounds like a return to the enigmatic bubbling swamp evoked earlier. At length, however, all that is left is a dense drone composed of organ and gliss guitar, above which – at the track's denouement – many cymbals sound, a hand drum patters and a keyboard bounces. The track ends with weird synths and more rapid-time echo effects, one of which seems to be a strangulated voice. Sonic enigma shrouds everything now – aimless organ, reverberated noises, sounds impossible to guess the origin of. This is the most effective and impressive track of the entire soundtrack – a terrific ending.

The main music of the year, however, was the second studio album *Alpha Centauri.* Recorded in January at Dieter Dierks' studio in Köln, the album itself was released a couple of months later, its arrival heralded by that most un-Tangerine-Dream of entities, a single: 'Ultima Thule Part 1'.

The band, at this point, had new members. One was organist Steve Schroyder, who, in a detailed interview given exclusively for this book, described those early days:

SP: What was your introduction to music when you were a young man?
SS: It began very early. As a kid of three or four, I was very fascinated by music. We were listening to old records from operas and other classic stuff, and I liked this very much. We had a piano in our home, and so at five, I began piano lessons. Even before I went to school, I tried to read musical notation: the score. I could read this before I could read letters. I was always impressed by my sister, who was six years older than me; she played the piano. I was eager to do the same stuff.
SP: Were you always drawn to keyboard instruments?
SS: Not only them, but to other things too. We had other musical instruments. I was always impressed by the sitar. My grandma had an old sitar, I really liked it. The sitar has a wooden resonator, which is fantastic. When you listen to the sitar, the resonance is amazing. I was fascinated by this. I was fascinated by radio music of all kinds. In the fifties – this

would be 1953 or 1954 – I heard a lot of music on German radio which was played by the Trautonium, as it had been in the 1930s. This has a special sound. When I remember this music, there was one piece I really liked, but I don't know the name. The sound was so amazing ... but the sounds on radio nowadays are very different. When I heard that kind of music, even with my parents, it was the first time we heard beat music or rock 'n' roll. There was one radio show on Sunday evening when the whole family was lying in bed and listening to this show. My mother too was very musical. She sang and played harmonica. I think it was because of that that I liked music. Our family liked music, but that did not come out of professional music. It was a very bourgeois feeling – taking the good parts of music and allowing the kids to grow up with music so they can play an instrument. My father was a watchmaker and he had a workshop, and there were all these clocks and watches, always ticking, ticking, ticking ... I really liked this and I spent hours there, listening to this ticking, it was great!

SP: Sound is very important to you.

SS: Yes! When we talk about it, the sound is more important than the melody, I would say.

SP: Did you know Edgar Froese or any of the early members of Tangerine Dream before you worked with them?

SS: No. I didn't know them personally. I first saw Tangerine Dream in 1968 at the Essener Songtage festival. It was spectacular. It was very unusual. They (festival people) cut their wires and they couldn't play on. The political students didn't like the sound because they thought music has to be political. They didn't want to waste time with this group! They just cut something – I don't know what happened. But the group just carried on acoustically, just singing, just making a chorus at the front of the stage. The students were trying to shut them down. This really impressed me.

SP: How did you come to work with Edgar Froese and the band?

SS: I had a very strong experience with LSD. It was a very nice experience. Then I came back to Germany, and something was telling me from space what to do – like an inner voice. It was telling me things: do this, do this, do this, you know? Or ... the little men in the lamp telling you things ... So, this was an idea of the inner voice telling me: 'You have to make music now'. I had a school band in my youth, where I was singing and even writing my own songs. I lived in a village before, but now I was living in Berlin, and this was a complete change for me for sure. I just came to Berlin to study, but I changed completely when I arrived. I was a political student in the 1968 movement, and went on demos on the street and things like this, and talked about things in discussion rounds (at university). In winter 1968, I went to India with a friend of mine, but we did not return for the next semester. We were jailed in Turkey for no reason. There was a little incident which could be misunderstood ... So I couldn't come back to university, I had to wait another half year. So with all the influences, I felt, like from India, I just felt I had to learn to break out of everything. I learned this somehow in India. This changed my life completely. I remember I had my own band before Tangerine Dream: it was called Turning Free. There were a lot of bands named Free ... like Agitation Free ... the word 'free' was very important I think. So I had some time in Berlin, and this voice was telling me, 'Look for Tangerine Dream, they have no keyboard player and they are looking for one!'. This voice knew what it said ... it was true! I didn't know this by the newspapers or something. I have thought so often about this since then, it's amazing. 'Okay', I said, 'Let's look'. I went to the record store to find out the address of Tangerine Dream, and I first went to Klaus Schulze. But he said, 'Oh no, I'm not with Tangerine Dream anymore, you have to go to Edgar'. 'Okay', I said ... My first meeting with Edgar was in Schwäbische Street. I rang the bell and looked up at the window on the fourth floor. Edgar said, 'Who's that?', and I said, 'Well, I'm your new keyboard player'. I said something like, 'I'm sent from space'. He said, 'Woah, that's good! How did you know?'. And he came down immediately and took me up in the elevator, and he was asking me, 'How did you know that we need someone?'. I said, 'Well, a voice out of space told me that'. So the ice was broken very soon!

SP: What was your first impression of Edgar Froese?

SS: He was really friendly. It was easy talking with him. We were really both like children ... not thinking *around,* but thinking *through,* and talking with no thoughts behind. I always laughed talking with Edgar. We had fantastic talks together. I liked to sit around with him and have a smoke, have a drink, you know, and to talk: about time, and space, and about music. This was the most important part of Tangerine Dream – not so much the music, more *around* the music.

SP: What can you tell me about the recordings for the album *Alpha Centauri*?

SS: It was all in one room, a very small room, not like the big room we had one year later with *Zeit.* We had to build a small room for Udo

Dennebourg – he had to work inside mattresses, inside the studio room! Chris still had his drum set. It was around the time he changed from drums to synthesizers. He stopped playing drums after *Alpha Centauri* – what he did on the album was just the drums. We were all very close, sitting together in this circle, and then we tried to make music like we did in Berlin in the rehearsal sessions or in the few live gigs that we did before that. It was like Chris and me and Edgar when we met for the first time. I always remember one thing about how we started, which gave me so much for my musical awareness – Edgar turned out the light so it was totally dark. We only had a few lamps on the keyboards. Then Edgar said, 'Shhh! We have to be quiet. We have to be very quiet. Slow down and listen *in* to the silence, and let the sound come out of the silence. Let it happen ... what you hear'. For me it was very special. My organ was more like a record player – a machine built in space, supported with tapes – I just pushed the buttons and sounds came out. That was how I played, actually! I had nothing in mind ... I felt I really had to *lose* my piano lessons. I spent two months all by myself in a house in Berlin Wannsee, where I only had the organ, and I tried to find new sounds and new harmonies in order to lose everything that I had learned before. I liked this very much! I liked Edgar's instruction very much – 'Please shut up, no sound! Listen to the silence ... Don't make the sound, when it comes it's good' ... But in the studio, it was very hard to keep this feeling with all the stresses around. You know ... the producer arrives and talks nonsense into your ears! I didn't know about this, and it was very hard for me to bear, this whole studio thing. The second time, it was even worse. So I left Tangerine Dream, walking right out of the room. It was not what I wanted in music. But nobody could foresee the success of *Alpha Centauri*. I didn't care about things like that. What I heard in the studio – and my feelings especially about making music together with musicians – made me leave. I imagined a free music somehow out of the formal music system. There was a misunderstanding with Chris as well ... and Paulick: this guy whose first time it was there. But the first moment was really great in the studio.

SP: Do you listen now to that album?

SS: Yes! For twenty years I couldn't listen to it, but I begin to like it now. I couldn't listen to it earlier, not because of the music, but because of the circumstances. Now I can listen to it and begin to like it somehow. A lot of people told me it's a really great album.

SP: So you do like the album now?

SS: I really had to go, you know. I left. But it was such a decision – I really had to go. I often think about it now, how it would have been if I had done other things, not relating to my inner wishes.

The other newcomers were flautist Udo Dennebourg and keyboards man Roland Paulick. However, neither of them stayed for long, and soon Froese and Franke were a duo again, albeit with somebody of great significance in the wings.

Alpha Centauri (1971)

Personnel:
Edgar Froese: guitar, organ, bass
Christopher Franke: drums, percussion, flute, zither, piano, VCS3 synthesizer
Steve Schroyder: organ, voice, echo machines, iron stick
Udo Dennebourg: flute, voice
Roland Paulick: synthesizer
Producer: Tangerine Dream and Dieter Dierks
Recorded at Dieter Dierks Studio, Köln: January 1971
Release date: March 1971
Chart placings: -
Running time: 39:48
All tracks by Tangerine Dream
Side One: 1. 'Sunrise In The Third System' 2. 'Fly And Collision Of Comas Sola'
Side Two: 1. 'Alpha Centauri'

After the jam session sounds, squally guitar feedback and heavy drumming of the debut LP, this follow-up album was far spacier, though evoking again the late 1960s work of Pink Floyd. The dominant timbres were keyboards, organs and the flute, here played by new member Udo Dennebourg. A crucial addition to the lineup, however, was the youthful Christopher Franke – only eighteen at the time of recording; a brilliant drummer amongst many other talents. (Schulze had departed the band to pursue a solo career, which would in a few years flourish and expand into a series of extraordinary, trailblazing albums.) *Alpha Centauri* set the tone for the next three years: spacey excursions, drifting textures, with the emphasis on keyboards.

'Sunrise In The Third System' opens the album. A plucked zither sounds in solitude, evoking the first hints of dawn on the horizon. As Froese's guitar brings in a meandering theme, a subtle, hallucinatory keyboard underpins the whole, until some well-judged gliss guitar (also evoking Pink Floyd – the effect was developed by Syd Barrett) adds new texture to the piece. This is definitely an alien system, though, as the vibe is entirely off-planet. An oscillating VCS3 synth brings mysterious tones to the listener as the organ changes mood and key. Light – evoked so well by the organ – is now brightening the sky. With it come new synth noises and the arrival of the flute, giving the impression of life activating itself to welcome the sun. Although this is an early piece of ***kosmische musik***, as the style would become known, it has a strong, even assured quality. The band knew what they were doing and what they wanted to achieve.

'Fly And Collision Of Comas Sola' – a much longer excursion – opens with sharp, heavily-reverberated VCS3 oscillating, accentuating the spacey vibe, until a muted drone accompaniment enters the mix. For some time these elements carry the listener through their sparse soundscape, before an organ playing a simple chord sequence comes into play, bringing a semblance of musicality amidst all the cosmic effects. This organ is reminiscent of the Pink Floyd track 'A Saucerful Of Secrets', both in tone and structure. Above it, however, the listener again hears rambling flute and metallic guitar chords, providing a different, albeit still psychedelic, mood.

As the chord sequence loops, new elements arrive, though none do much to alter the overall spacious effect. This is a music of solemn stasis, describing an environment of glacial splendour.

Eventually, all that is left are great swathes of oscillating VCS3 synth, and the circling, cycling organ, which serves at once to anchor the listener but also convey them across the vastness of space. These main elements come together in a great blaze of sound, the majesty of stars in deep blackness, and us, tiny and insignificant before them.

But at length, the planet beckons – Franke's drums pound, and the guitar and flute return. Now the flute plays a recognisable solo over the same chord sequence, this time transmuted into a planetside psychedelic jam, in which the band bring all the elements together to work in synchrony. Franke is particularly strong here – pounding the tom-toms and crashing the cymbals to terrific effect – though the flute remains to guide the listener.

At length, however, the drums fade, the mood lifts, and what remains is steady heartbeat drums, much reverberation, and a ghost of the organ and VCS3. Reverberation conveys distance: the music is departing. Suddenly, it is gone.

Some say this track ends naturally; others say the tape ran out...

The title track takes up all of side B, opening with spacey effects in VCS3 style. Reverberation mixes this melange of weird effects, conveying an atmosphere of space and dark vistas. As the music progresses, a simple organ chord emerges from the mix, accompanied by a half-melodic/half-random keyboard line, which is itself overtaken by a wandering flute.

For some time, the listener is transported through this environment, which, though it does transmute and change, does so slowly and over long periods. This is an unhurried journey, with plenty of time to take in the view. Some effects have much vibrato applied to them, while others are great cosmic glissandos on unknown instruments, reverberated and dense, as is every sound here. At length, however, something brand new does arrive – a looping guitar figure repeated alongside a VCS3 wail, to which Dennebourg's flute is applied. It is as though a human newcomer has arrived in the depths of space. The flute then takes the lead, alongside it more gliss guitar, as if on some strange, meandering journey – and this part of the journey is lengthy, taking us to the halfway point.

Without warning, a completely new element appears – a German voice, intoning a slightly distorted liturgy, as of some weird radio broadcast transmitted through deep space. The flute continues underneath, but now the mood is wholly changed. The gliss guitar sounds much more ominous, mutated into a strange electric breath.

Following the spoken voice come a pair of singing voices – Schroyder and Dennebourg – in a style very much like the ending of 'A Saucerful Of Secrets'. The vibe is of some reverential service, accompanied by the organ's church-like tones. More VCS3 is added to this music, giving the section its spacey element, until the music fades, leaving just the organ echoes. As the voices also fade, all that is left is reverberant silence.

Alpha Centauri proved to be a turning point in Froese's concept of where he wanted to go with Tangerine Dream. The group – now recording in a proper studio, with time to experiment, getting their keyboard sounds exactly as they wanted them – did not have to rely on an old two-track Revox tape recorder: Dierks' studio had an eight-track recorder. The release schedule, too, was also a little more ambitious, Ohr deciding to release the LP outside Germany, in France and America.

Although the group membership was still not quite settled (Schroyder departed in February, one month after recording the album), a significant addition was about to be made in the shape of Peter Baumann. Baumann in fact made his first recording with Froese and Franke on 'Ultima Thule.' At the time, this related cut – a four-minute piece – was released as a heavy single called 'Ultima Thule Part 1', using distorted guitar, drums and bass to rocking effect, mimicking the wilder moments of Pink Floyd. The musical material sounds in places not unlike that of *Alpha Centauri*, but with a far more psychedelic sound. Again Franke's drumming is central to the track's pounding beat and propulsive motion. The irony is that this rock cut was about as far as it was possible to get from the album's main mood – and in fact from the group's career after *Electronic Meditation.*

Baumann, however, turned out to be a fixture and a brilliant one at that. A resident of Berlin and part of the band Burning Touch, he was a self-taught musician with great facility on keyboards, as can be seen and heard in the Ossiach Lake film fragment. In the LP liner notes, Baumann is credited under his full name: Hans Peter Baumann.

In an April 2020 interview with Danny Scott at *musicradar.com*, Baumann recalled how he was introduced to Tangerine Dream:

> (It was) a complete accident. I was at a concert, and I ended up talking to this guy who turned out to be Christopher Franke. I told him that I was playing in a band but I didn't find the music exciting. It was a covers band ... playing English and US rock covers. I told him that I wanted to find something that was more experimental. He seemed quite excited by this and made a note of my address. Several days later, I received a letter asking me to come to a rehearsal. His band was looking for a keyboard player ... This was decades before mobile phones. In fact, I didn't even have a normal phone ... Musicians didn't make much money back then!

Baumann recalled how uncertain he was before that first meeting:

> When I went along to see them, I was worried that they thought I was some kind of master keyboard player. I wasn't! I grew up with classical music, because my father was a composer, and yes, I understood classical music, but I wasn't a fantastic classical musician. There was no need for me to worry. When I arrived at the studio, I said, 'Okay, what are we playing? What's the song?'. Edgar said, 'I don't know what we're playing. We'll start something and you can join in with us'. Christopher was brushing the cymbals very gently, and Edgar started to create these long eerie sounds with the guitar ... The early songs were often created with guitars, organs, tape loops and heavy use of effect boxes. I listened to the mood of the music and thought, 'What do I play?'. That was kind of how Tangerine Dream evolved. It was all about the mood of the music.

In an interview in issue 14 of *Prog* magazine, Baumann recalled the Berlin music scene of the time: '(We did not feel part of the scene) at all. The Amon Düül guys and the Kraftwerk guys felt like they were all isolated. We were totally self-absorbed. There wasn't much hanging out at all'.

In the same interview, Froese explained this sensation of separation:

> There was a strong musical community in Germany during that period, but we weren't a part of it. We couldn't even invite others for a jam session ... because when we were switching on the knobs, everybody became very suspicious ... There was one experience during a gig in Berlin with Amon Düül II; before we started, I gave the keynote of our philosophy, by saying, 'Dear friends, it's December 6th 1971 at 8 pm in the city of West Berlin. Please be kind enough to improvise with us in a way that never can be repeated'. They stared at me as if I had taken my head off and put it under my arm.

In the interview, Baumann recalled the dynamics of the group:

> It was strange. When the three of us were together, it felt like there was a fourth person there, a fourth energy ... We felt like we didn't have personal profiles, we were a unit. We'd get together and stay up all night and listen to music – from Italian classical music to the first Pink Floyd record. We never watched TV; we'd just hang out, smoke a joint and listen to music until the early hours of the morning.

In the 2020 interview given to Danny Scott at musicradar.com, Baumann gave a fascinating insight into what it was like working with Froese:

> Edgar did not get excited too often. Upset, yes! At the record company, the promoter ... In the studio and in general, he was very cool, calm and collected. It was very easy to work with Edgar. He didn't complain much in the studio, and was happy with most of what we created together. His mind was always drawn to the edge ... the edge of science, beliefs, consciousness and the edge of music.

Thus it was that the group devoted themselves to the music they loved. But there was change brewing, which in the not-too-distant future would reveal itself through the instruments the group chose to make their music with. A cosmic paradigm change was on the way.

1972 – Concerts, Time, Keyboards

As the year progressed, keyboards and synthesizers became the dominant mode of musical expression within Tangerine Dream. With the success of *Alpha Centauri* improving on that of the group's debut, and with Rolf-Ulrich Kaiser's Ohr Records as keen as ever to release their music, the trio of Froese, Franke and Baumann returned to Dieter Dierks' Köln studio in May 1972 to record what would become the immense work released as the double LP *Zeit.*

There were still guest musicians around, however, the trio not quite working alone as a stable unit. One of those musicians was Steve Schroyder, making a final visit before vanishing for good. Of equal significance was Florian Fricke of Popol Vuh.

By 1972, Popol Vuh had released two albums of trailblazing electronic music: *Affenstunde* and *In Den Gärten Pharaos*. The band were a respected underground entity, with Fricke a unique figure in music – iconoclastic, spiritual, somehow apart in his desire to create 'hymnical music' or 'shamanism music' as he called it. But for Tangerine Dream, the most significant aspect of Fricke's involvement in helping to record *Zeit* was that he owned a Moog III synthesizer.

Much has been made of this instrument and the way it became part of the group. In 1971 in Germany, only Fricke and Eberhard Schoener possessed such an exotic thing. Created by the American electronics expert Robert Moog, one of its earliest appearances had been on the Sagittarius LP *The Blue Marble*, where – used by Gary Usher, who had been introduced to it by Roger McGuinn of The Byrds – it contributed to the album's unique timbre. Usher, however, not in the best psychological health at the time and struggling to get to grips with the Moog, on his own admission used the synthesizer to mediocre effect. Fricke on the other hand was already using the Moog to create a unique sound palette, which – on *Affenstunde* in particular – paved the way for what would become fully-fledged electronic music.

In Danny Scott's interview at musicradar.com, Baumann recalled the arrival of synthesizers:

> Suddenly, synths seemed to be ... around. More people had them. In the beginning, it was baby steps. The first synth I ever saw was so basic: just a box with one knob that switched from pink noise to white noise. And I don't think any of us really worried about how much synthesizers were

> going to change the musical landscape. We didn't feel like revolutionaries ... Today, we're using a guitar and Farfisa organ. Tomorrow, we'll be using synthesizers. Fine. No problem. These new instruments were available, so we decided to use them.

One synth in particular – used by Pink Floyd to marvellous effect on *The Dark Side Of The Moon* – became a staple of the early group sound: the VCS3, made by EMS. In the *musicradar.com* interview, Baumann remembered it well:

> The machine that really got things going for us was the EMS Synthi, which came from England. If you want to talk about a revolution, this was the point that it started. We began to understand what these new machines could offer us ... We wanted to make music that was different to the music our parents listened to. The synthesizer seemed to capture the new spirit. It wasn't the blues. It wasn't rock music. It wasn't about playing these incredible solos. It was a new era.

The recording sessions for *Zeit* also marked a change for Froese and Franke. In his 1980 interview with *Neumusik*, Froese recalled that time: 'That was a big step, because that's when I gave up playing the guitar. Peter Baumann joined the band, and Chris didn't want to play drums anymore'.

Other guests included four cellists, used to spine-tingling effect at the beginning of the first movement 'Birth Of Liquid Plejades', about which Froese spoke in the same interview: 'They were four students. All they had to play was A-440, and just vary one quarter-tone out of it'.

The tenor of the music recorded that year was icy and slow, lacking most elements of melody and rhythm. When *Zeit* was released in August, there was, at the time, almost nothing like it.

Zeit (1972)

Personnel:

Edgar Froese: audio generators, gliss guitar

Chris Franke: keyboards, VCS3 synthesizer, cymbals

Peter Baumann: organ, vibraphone, VCS3 synthesizer

Steve Schroyder: organ

Florian Fricke: Moog synthesizer ('Birth Of Liquid Plejades')

The Cologne Cello Quartet: Christian Vallbracht, Joachim von Grumbkow, Hans

Joachim Brüne and Johannes Lücke ('Birth of Liquid Plejades')
Producer: Tangerine Dream and Dieter Dierks
Recorded at Dieter Dierks Studio, Köln: May 1972
Release date: August 1972
Chart placings: -
Running time: 74:29
All tracks by Froese, Franke, Baumann
Side One: 1. 'Birth Of Liquid Plejades'
Side Two: 1. 'Nebulous Dawn'
Side Three: 1. 'Origin Of Supernatural Probabilities'
Side Four: 1. 'Zeit'

The album opens with the thrilling sound of four cellos playing in unison, with each slight variation in pitch and texture adding to the overall effect. There is no explanation for this, no development – just the sound itself. It is already a depiction of the temporal world, a philosophy Froese considered to be based on the notion that time (zeit) is motionless, existing only in our minds. As new notes enter the mix, the sound – a kind of ever-repeating chord, permanently cycling – becomes fuller, albeit with the same mood and timbre, modified only by phasing at the end. This section lasts for seven wonderful minutes before fading.

The opening movement's second section – the album was subtitled *Largo In Four Movements* – returns the group to the keyboards of earlier LPs, this time augmented by VCS3 synthesizer bleeps and whirrs. The tone is glacial, movement hardly perceptible: sparse, spacey, distant. We are in space, a fact alluded to by the 1970s space font used for the band name and album title on the front cover. Brief inserts of gliss guitar arrive from time to time, but everything is underpinned by the permanent, revolving organ drone, which dominates the sonic spectrum. This is an evocation of the sheer scale of space – its expanse, its emptiness.

The third section is also organ-dominated, but the shimmering tone does add a little movement to the mix, albeit in a never-varying rhythmic pattern, which itself echoes the perpetual cycling of time. Phasing effects alter the mix, and again there are ghostly echoes of gliss guitar, but still the mood is icy and spacious. This is, however, a slightly fuller sound than the middle section's cold abstract sheen. There are also chord changes, though few and far between.

The second track 'Nebulous Dawn' opens with doomy, threatening bass drones and a slowly cycling synth tone, which keeps to the same note and rhythm. As the thrumming drone increases, new effects fade in and out of the mix, until an amplified and echoed white noise effect brings some small sense of movement. Chimes and electronic squeals from the VCS3 synthesizer augment the mix, giving an impression of space, yet near some colossal object, which, without cease, continues to broadcast its cycling synth tone.

As the music develops, new synth sounds emerge, one hinting at structure: a new cycling pattern based on two notes. These new sounds and effects vary over long periods, again hinting at the immensity of the time scale of the universe. It is as if the music is describing the ten billion years before the arrival of our sun and earth.

More variation in the white noise bubbles bring a new timbre, but still, movement is barely noticeable – sonic drift. The background and much of the foreground is nearly static. Slow change forces the mind to perceive time as it is. Much of this track follows the synth timbre of Klaus Schulze's *Cyborg* album released the same year: remote, cold, hardly human.

'Origin Of Supernatural Probabilities' opens with a soft series of repeating guitar chords, conspicuously more human than the keyboard sounds which preceded it. After a while, whirring, whining synth effects emerge, alongside a few VCS3 bubbles.

The second section is ushered in with floating gliss guitar: a rich sound given life with lots of delay. As bassy oscillating keyboard textures begin to arrive, the mood changes to one of organic, yet alien, life – enigmatic, unknowable. Yet even this life is almost static, oscillating on its own time scale, endlessly; a complete mystery. Perhaps the music is depicting the slow heartbeat of an entire planet. This section does develop, however, as a whooping synth sound echoes across alien plains. The bass drones now mimic volcanic events, the low register gliss guitar the ash-filled, unearthly skies. We are somewhere impossible to comprehend; a place of immense time scales.

As new, harsher gliss and synth effects emerge into the mix, a sense of slow, doomy change begins to unfold. There is motion here, albeit on an incomprehensible scale. It is a reminder that the human scale is short and sweet. Space and time operate on entirely different templates.

The title track is similarly enigmatic and cold. Beginning with phased effects and another slowly-repeating VCS3 pattern, the piece floats dark and vast in free space. As a subtle gliss guitar phrase repeats over droning keyboards, that single sound is the only acknowledgement of something other than endless, spacious night. It admits one listener, giving them the sparsest of sonic vehicles in which to travel. Everything else is of the universe.

This music is huge, eternal. It could be played forever on a loop, describing the very universe it inhabits. Nobody could remember it in its entirety, giving it an essential enigma.

Zeit is often regarded as Tangerine Dream's most difficult album, but taken on its own terms, it is a brilliant piece of music. As a description of slow change, of universal space themes and of the endlessly repeating nature of astronomical time, it captures the heart of the experience: vast, impenetrable, inhuman, chilled.

This album marked the opening statement in Tangerine Dream's electronic music forays. Though other instruments were used during its recording, its reliance on keyboards and synthesizers was to become a mainstay of the group's sound, not least because synths allowed the trio to make music entirely unlike the rock 'n' roll and psychedelic rock of their peers and parents. An evolutionary musical step was being taken.

David Elliott and Wolfgang Fenchel interviewed Chris Franke for *Neumusik* fanzine, where Franke spoke about that time and the reason for him changing to play keyboards:

> When I started working with experimental music and electronic sound sources in the form of collages or loop techniques and so on, I was trying to get a bigger spectrum of sounds from my drum sets. They were already pretty sophisticated with experimental sound sources, but I still wasn't satisfied with the possibilities of expressing the sounds I had in mind. So when I came into contact with electronics, I saw a much wider range of things which I could express. Later, I changed to be more and more a designer or creator or, as everybody says, a composer of music.

In the interview given for this book, Steve Schroyder described his memories of *Zeit*:

> SP: What do you remember about the album *Zeit*? How did you get involved in recording the first track, 'Birth Of Liquid Plejades'?
> SS: I left Tangerine Dream and looked for other things, but there were very bad circumstances where I ended up. So, I only had the chance to talk to Edgar in Berlin, half a year later or so. Edgar was really surprised

and happy to see me again. 'Hey', he said, 'You've got to play with us again! But, sorry, we had to pick another guy in the meantime, Peter Baumann'. I had lost my first organ, this very special instrument from space, with all this data from space inside. So I had to get a new one somehow. That first organ I had from my mother: she was preparing the way for me all the time. This second one was another Farfisa, but there wasn't such a musical feeling to it. Actually, I didn't play only on the first track, I played on most of the music on *Zeit*, but my part is a very small amount. 'Birth Of Liquid Plejades' is the piece with the Hammond organ. And they said, 'Steve, you have to play your organ like you did on *Alpha Centauri*!'. But it was a Hammond organ, and that was a mistake. I could better handle the Farfisa. So, for *Zeit*, I didn't feel so good with Hammond part. I thought, I climb up, I climb up, but I don't really reach the top; so I stayed somewhere and there's no evolution out of there ... but it's certainly a good view on my feelings on that day at that time. The studio at Dieter Dierks' was much bigger. We had the big Moog synthesizer there, it was very new.
SP: Was that the one which belonged to Florian Fricke?
SS: No. Florian Fricke brought his own. I really liked meeting him for that session! Florian and me were sharing one room in the studio, and this was really great. I had a good contact with Florian, and we had a lot of fun, while the others were rather nervous. Edgar was really so nervous through all the sessions, especially with the cello players all around.
SP: What do you remember about the Köln Cello Quartet?
SS: It took a really long time to record just this one note; such a long time that Florian and I were joking about it. It was somehow that we should play, but they had to record before we could play ... It was taking so long. Maybe because of that, Edgar was very nervous. He was always nervous about the future of Tangerine Dream, because nobody could tell him everything. I always told him, 'It's great, go on! It will be a great future!'.
SP: He was a very musical man, perhaps he was worried that all this wonderful music would be lost.
SS: Yes, I think so. But they didn't tell me anything, like, you're back in the group or you're not back in the group. Nothing really was said, so that situation was not bearable for me. I couldn't make a contact with Peter. With Christopher, I couldn't warm to him from the beginning onward. I liked him somehow, but he just played drums on *Alpha Centauri*, and for a lot of the album, he didn't have anything to do.

> Perhaps I didn't respect him as much as I should have respected him.
> SP: Any other memories? What about Dieter Dierks?
> SS: Dierks was a rock 'n' roll freak! He had no idea about this music. Maybe it would have been good if we'd joined Conny Plank. He had an idea about sound. I think he was better for all the groups playing electronic music in those days. But I met Dierks again with Ash Ra Tempel – *Seven Up* – and the after-production we made at Dierks' with Manuel, Dierks and other studio musicians. He had really good ideas, especially for the *Seven Up* album with Ash Ra Tempel – the first side is like rock 'n' roll, you know? Technical-wise, he is very professional for sure.

As if to underline the steps taken on *Zeit*, on 25 November the group played their first ever concert using nothing but electronic instruments, although it seems likely that Froese did return to his gliss guitar that night, probably played through a volume-swell pedal to make it sound less like an ordinary guitar. Made at the broadcasting studio of television station WDR in Köln, the concert lasted for almost an hour and is now publicly (non-commercially) available.

The music opens with white noise and industrial sounds, an oscillating synth entering the mix not long after, underpinned by dense drones and a pulsing bass note. Taking their cue from the drone pitch, other keyboards arrive, including an organ with a vaguely 1960s feel, though it is played with a wah pedal. Soon the tempo of the thrumming bass note quickens, and now the music has an urgent feel to it. The organ line turns into more of a solo, before a second, more choral organ, sounds. Much has been made of Pink Floyd's influence on Froese, but this is perhaps the first music to simultaneously evoke the more cosmic aspects of that band and yet be something very different. It is extraordinarily atmospheric.

As the thrum fades, a cosmic organ shimmers alone in deep space before a melancholy sound arrives – most likely Froese's gliss guitar – and with it, a new bass drone. Later, various hallucinatory keyboard sounds enter the mix as if describing new regions of deep space littered with dust and debris. With the new synths comes a new rhythmic element, acquired through echo and some reverberation. The key of the music has changed; some elements aligned, others off-kilter. This seems to be a passage of motion through space, evoked with oscillating VCS3 sounds and a hint of organ. As this second section comes to a conclusion, the VCS3 chatter takes on an almost vocal quality, as if describing alien speech.

The third part of the concert opens with a new organ sound playing new chords. While the VCS3 chatter fades, other echoed sounds continue before they too fade. This section conveys some of the atmosphere of *Alpha Centauri* through its use of reverberated organ chords and notes in particular: an almost church-like sonic environment. Then the music returns the listener to filtered white noise and other enigmatic sounds, all fed through a massive echo unit. There is some audience applause here, indicating a move from part one of the live event to part two.

The next new section is based on a simple drone, ghostly synth notes, and a plucked keyboard sound not unlike a harpsichord: perhaps a clavinet or equivalent. As the spectral notes lengthen and reveal their origin in the VCS3 synth, the music starts to coalesce around the drone as if evoking the preparations for some arcane procession. Now the clavinet part is more of a solo: sometimes complex, sometimes just a series of dense chords. A new chord forces this solo into a new, atonal key, and suddenly the music is uncomfortable; though, in due course, the chords return to a major key before being given the time and space to elaborate upon it. Eventually, however, as with previous sections, the music dissociates into VCS3 noise and strange deeply-reverberated sounds.

The concert's concluding section is, at its beginning, based around a pair of organ chords and more VCS3 noise, which the group use as ever to evoke vast spaces and deep time. As the organ settles on one key, further keyboards emerge, and then the VCS3 acquires a fantastic upward-glissando, at once sinuous yet composed of separate notes. Soon this sound takes over the mix, before fading into reverb, the music now acquiring a dense, almost anthemic quality as volume and emotional intensity increase. When a rhythmic element begins (reminiscent of the Pink Floyd track 'One Of These Days'), the organ lines turn into a solo, which soon dissolves into other keyboards before being paired with a more sophisticated rhythmic synth. Though not created by a Moog, this element stands as one of the earliest expositions of the style the group would become famous for.

All in all, this concert shows the group in superb form: confident, evocative, atmospheric. This is not the Tangerine Dream of the previous two years – struggling to find their voice and master the techniques of their instruments – the compositional style alone showing a group in charge of its musical destiny.

A recording also exists of a similar concert, titled *Klangwald Köln WDR Sendesaal, Deutschland,* and catalogued in the fan recordings as Tangerine Tree TT52. This recording is of excellent quality and was commercially released in 2012, mastered by Wouter Bessels, as part of Esoteric Recordings' *Zeit* reissue. It stands as a terrific example of the glacial mood of the music the group was making in 1972.

The first part opens with an eerie yet ominous drone, soon augmented by white noise and some kind of metallic synth. As further sounds bubble up in the mix, the music turns even darker, as if describing macabre weather: the onset of a storm. Yet that storm never arrives, as the music journeys elsewhere into spacier environments with more cosmic weather, evoked in the main by a church organ. Now the drone is even deeper: a single dense note anchoring the whole improvisation. As a new keyboard enters, an unearthly voice (it doesn't sound like a synthesizer or gliss guitar) appears from far away – it's impossible to conceive it, as if the voice's owner is floating alone in deep space and has been for eons. Around it, VCS3 fragments oscillate; an alien counterpoint. This voice hovers, swoops and dives as the organ and VCS3 acquire emotional intensity, at times the bass voice of a man, but eventually, it fades into the cosmic mélange of sound, along with its accompanying synth.

The next section arrives with a gentler keyboard sound – perhaps an early string synthesizer (e.g. the Logan) – against which a VCS3 pattern oscillates and the organ whirrs. The effect is soothing; much more earthly than the preceding section. Later sections evoke terrestrial weather – pattering raindrops, the drone of distant winds, the occasional thrum of thunder. It is like a distant storm: dangerous, yes, but far off near the horizon.

When a new organ sounds – this time much more like the church keyboard used earlier – a new optimism arrives. The tone of the music is almost hopeful, again supported by string-flavoured keyboards (though not a Mellotron, I suspect) and light VCS3 twitter. This is the music of some planetside ritual, albeit from a country the listener is unfamiliar with. When a rhythmic thrum enters the mix, the music acquires forward motion, as of ritual changed into procession.

Soon though, all that is left is the thrum – now quite macabre in timbre – and weird keyboard fragments. Suddenly, the music is much darker, as if describing a kind of ritualistic madness. The keyboard solo becomes harsh, sometimes atonal, stopping and starting, then vanishing without warning. When the pulse becomes percussive in tone, the listener seems to be in the centre of a ritual, half-tribal/half-alien, with only the organ whirring in the background and a few high-pitched synth warbles for company. Something wild and primitive is evoked here: ancient ritual, dense, intense. At length, the tribal rhythm mutates and fades, to be replaced by a solitary organ hum and some VCS3 chatter.

The music's second part opens with an eerie, high modulating keyboard line, evoking something isolated, mournful, even tragic. Subtle VCS3 twitter accompanies this sound: hardly audible, like birdsong long-lost. After a while, an understated organ emerges, yet it also is hardly audible. The mood is melancholy in the extreme, yet not entirely cold; this does seem to be music evoking something human.

In due course, the music becomes a tranquil, slowly-changing sonic drift of cold, isolated parts; a trio entwined, yet at astronomical distances. This is very much the mood of the album *Zeit*. The listener is in interstellar space: nothing nearby. Only stars and dust accompany them. It is at least as brilliant an evocation of the vast reaches of space as anything on the LP, highlighted by the beautiful way the parts accompany one another in ever looser sonic attachment, until all that is left is a bass thrum and vague hints of what sounded before.

Eventually, the music acquires a hint of structure, as slowly-progressing chords accompany a high-register organ, itself accompanied by a gliss guitar using wide, intense vibrato. Then a new form arrives: strummed guitar chords, not unlike those opening *Zeit*'s third side. This again returns the listener to the human world, perhaps a lone astral traveller. It is almost comforting.

At the end of the drift, two new themes appear – one a bright, chiming synth sound, the other a series of dense keyboard washes – alternately thrumming and fading, like an audio tide. Soon though, these are replaced by a three-note keyboard riff and bass-heavy noise, which itself is counterpointed in a high register by VCS3 warbles. The mood is of anticipation, yet it is not frightening, only eerie. At length, only the warbles and a thin mutation of the organ remain.

This mood of weird reflection continues for quite a while, at last accompanied by a rhythmic bass sound that intensifies the mood. Then Froese's electric guitar comes into play, providing glissandos akin to those used on *Alpha Centauri*, before, just as quickly, they depart. But suddenly the bass thrum acquires urgency, its tempo increasing, as the organ shimmers and oscillates around it. This is the end of the concert, and all elements combine; urgency, intensity, organs, keyboards and VCS3 whistles. As the bass thrum changes into a two-note sequence, the mood is dominated by a sense of fear, as of some approaching terror.

When the organ turns into church mode, that sense intensifies still further; distortion adding to its awesome sound. The organ now fully describes the approaching entity: something huge and terrible. Yet, not for long does this terror last. In due course the tension relaxes as new keyboard sounds emerge; then the bass note halts, lengthens and increases in pitch...

Which is where the music fades, alas. A terrific ending to a wonderful concert.

The band played at least nine dates in Germany as the months passed, but by the end of the year their focus was on a new album. In December, Froese, Franke and Baumann returned to Dieter Dierks' studio to begin recording what would the following year be their breakthrough work. The world was beginning to notice Tangerine Dream.

1973 – Keyboards, Peel, Success

The year of *The Dark Side Of The Moon*, of *Tales From Topographic Oceans*, and of Klaus Schulze's *Blackdance* would also prove transformative for Tangerine Dream. As 1972 slipped into 1973, recording for the album *Atem* continued at Dieter Dierks' Köln studio, the emphasis this time on music less remote, less forbidding, more approachable.

In an interview given to *Melody Maker* in October 1994, Froese recalled the studio atmosphere at the time:

> *Atem* was the beginning of an adventure. For the next few years, we were constantly improving and experimenting, and although it wasn't perfect – we didn't always make great music – it was a period which brought me richer experiences than any other.

There were no guests on the recordings, the now stable trio of Froese, Franke and Baumann happy to work together. There was, however, friction between the group and Ohr's Rolf-Ulrich Kaiser, which in due course would mean the group departing from the label following a lawsuit. *Atem*, released in March, would be the final album of the so-called pink years on Ohr.

But by now, Tangerine Dream – with four albums, plenty of concerts and festival appearances under their belts, and an enthusiastic underground following – were making a name for themselves outside their home nation. In Britain, one man in particular would lead the group to global success through his efforts. His name was John Peel.

In fact, his real name was John Ravenscroft, but to his legions of devoted fans he was just Peel – the great man on BBC Radio who played the kind of music they loved. John Peel's entry into radio was – as is so often the case in creative circles – a mixture of chance, luck and networking. A British journalist in America in the early 1960s, he was present at the assassination of Lee Harvey Oswald, making for himself a kind of career by associating his own Liverpool roots with that of The Beatles, then surfing the American wave of Beatlemania. In this manner, he acquired friends, contacts and kudos. Back in Britain for the cultural transformation of the mid-1960s, pirate radio and the Summer of Love, he was present at the founding of the BBC's new youth station Radio 1, which he subverted in his unmistakably droll manner, playing the dippiest of hippy tracks, and anything and everything else which took his fancy. Soon, he was a fixture, beloved of all true music fans, as indeed he is today. There was nobody like him, and there never will be again.

Peel had a particular taste for underground music, and when he heard a mysterious German album called *Atem* he was hooked. He loved it. It is thought he contacted Froese to tell him how much he loved the LP. In due course, Peel would make *Atem* his album of the year. Yet he was not the only foreign fan of Tangerine Dream: an American critic called John Schaeffer wrote in *New Sounds* in 1987, summarising the group's position and relevance at the time:

> Here were three young German rock musicians (Klaus Schulze briefly among them) playing music that sounded as bizarre and self-indulgent to pop listeners, as Eminent or Stockhausen sounded too much of the traditional classical audience. Often without any recognisable melodies or harmonies, the early Tangerine Dream recordings – such as the two-record set *Zeit* (Time) – took the listener on a flight through a chemical wonderland. Spaced, occasionally abrasive, at times completely adrift from conventional musical forms...

Atem was a move away from the glacial sound of *Zeit,* towards the more varied, human style of *Alpha Centauri.* Yet, in terms of composition, sound, variety and sheer style, it was a big step forward from that second album. *Atem* summarised what they had achieved in three years.

Atem (1973)

Personnel:
Edgar Froese: mellotron, organ, guitar, voice
Chris Franke: VCS3 synthesizer, drums, percussion, organ, voice
Peter Baumann: organ, piano, VCS3 synthesizer
Producer: Tangerine Dream and Dieter Dierks
Recorded at Dieter Dierks Studio, Köln: December 1972-January 1973
Release date: March 1973
Chart placings: -
Running time: 41:28
All tracks by Froese, Franke, Baumann
Side One: 1. 'Atem'
Side Two: 1. 'Fauni-Gena' 2. 'Circulation Of Events' 3. 'Wahn'

Like the title *Atem* – meaning breath – the album exudes the sound of breathing at its opening, a great in/out rush of synthesized musical air, below which a riff emerges to take stage centre alongside Franke's pounding drums. As the main theme develops and acquires a harmony, the noise of breathing is still evident, but now modulated through new synths and keyboard sounds. It is at once epic and massive, yet strangely personal if the listener keeps in mind that act of breathing.

The drums develop, becoming more intense as new layers of organ enter the mix, alternately shimmering and whirring, with a new keyboard riff oscillating on top. As the drums take up a double-speed rhythm, further layers are added, with new harmonies and new bass notes changing the key, then returning to it. Synths crackle and squeal; but below it all, the drums continue, pounding without cease, getting faster and faster, as the synth layers above them mutate, fade, then return with more organ. Just five minutes in, the music has an unbearable intensity, as of a great event about to occur – a rocket launch perhaps – evoked by those pounding drums and the whirring, whirling organ and keyboard sounds, now accentuated by a screaming VCS3 synth...

And then it suddenly stops.

All that is left are drifting organ chords and hints of deeply reverberated synths. The listener is somewhere out in space, with little to view, little to experience except their own breathing. As even this ghostly impression fades, the sound world is diminished still further, to a whirring organ and a tremulous keyboard: deep, dark space. Isolation, calm, stasis.

Slowly, new keyboard layers stack up, giving a clearer picture: space, still, but perhaps with the home planet in view. Stasis is replaced by slow movement, evoked by whirring organ and single keyboard notes, held for many seconds. All other sounds come from far away, indicated by their heavy reverberation.

Now a bass thrum begins, and strangely-echoed noises as of orbital footsteps – a visitor, perhaps. Over this, the layers of keyboards shimmer and drift, occasionally lifting in intensity, more often drifting into inaudibility. But the visitor continues to make their presence felt, the rhythm of their footsteps doubling-up in a 4/4 time signature.

When a new intensity begins – quite suddenly – it is accompanied by muffled groaning created by noisy keyboards, and a new urgency in the shimmering organ chords. Something is happening, some union of space traveller and visitor, the pair merging into a coherent whole, evoked by oscillating keyboards, bass drones and whirring effects, as of an approaching space vehicle. A distant keyboard sounds: a far off voice. Now the whirring intensifies, akin to an electronic helicopter as if the traveller and the visitor are returning to Earth through the moist, heavy weight of our atmosphere. New keyboard textures evoke wind and rain, and other weather – the noisy, chaotic march of the planet's air, evoked with ever more intense keyboard layers. There is noise, there is buffeting, but the descent continues, stately and certain, to a landing far below.

The landing is swift and successful: a few piano chords, a bit of a thunk, and that's it.

Side B has three cuts, opening with the eleven-minute audio excursion that is 'Fauni-Gena'. Here, the music evokes an alien landscape via oscillating high-pitched keyboards and meandering, heavily-reverberated Mellotron flutes. The mood is weird, sparse, half-eerie/half-homely – the noise of electric creatures contrasting with the human bedrock of the Mellotron.

But this landscape offers little by way of movement. It is vast, enigmatic, unchanging. Alterations of the keyboard sound evoke occasional differences in texture and climate, but overall the mood is one of stasis. Sometimes it is a stillness of Mellotron strings, at other times a haunting organ is the main keyboard. Over all this, the electric birds burble and twitter, occasionally answered by what seems to be a half-human voice, itself modified electronically through layers of delay.

As the Mellotron strings take centre stage, other keyboard layers come and go, but they rarely stay for long – and in the end, all that is left is thrumming noise and electric birdsong.

The track is like an audio description of the French animation film *Fantastic Planet* – released in the same year as this album – deeply odd, mysterious, unresolved.

'Circulation Of Events' is similar in tone and vibe, though with more of a psychedelic tinge. Again, drifting organ textures are to the fore, this time underpinned with shimmering drones. This is a mystical procession – very slow, very stately, entirely enigmatic. We do not know where we are or why we have come here, but the music evokes the mood perfectly. It is dense, ambiguous, without form.

Some sections of this six-minute piece have the feel of Pink Floyd's late 1960s experiments, though here there is more density, more depth, conveyed in the main by the use of throbbing drones. Most of the instruments cannot be identified: keyboards, sound modules, noise builders. As a new thrumming chord enters the mix, there is the hint of a reaction – electronic cries, perhaps of ancient gulls at a seashore –

until the thrum returns and the shimmering keyboard fades away. The procession has reached its endpoint.

'Wahn' is wholly unlike anything else on the album, or anything the group did before or after. The word 'wahn' means 'delusion' in German, and this is what the listener first hears – wordless, meaningless shouts of human voices, given depth and space through reverberation and echo. It is a complex, mystic opening ritual to some occurrence we know is going to be heavy and devastating.

And soon, that event occurs. With terrifying drums – also echoed – the voices acquire anguish, pain, as if describing the terror of madness: the full depth of delusion. As the drums take over, pounding away as on the title track, a lone wailing voice acts as the bridge from human madness to musical madness. Mellotrons swarm this way and that, accompanied by harmonising keyboards, all the time underpinned by the headlong, chaotic, pounding beat of Franke's drums.

But after a couple of minutes the delusion begins to pass, as the humane Mellotron flute emerges, playing a wandering melody, bringing a human face to wipe madness away. As the music ebbs, all that is left is a psychedelic, clinking keyboard and the remains of the Mellotron. The delusion is over.

Many elements of earlier music were brought together in this album – Franke's drumming, the use of multi-layered keyboards, exotic synth sounds and the distinctive timbres of the Mellotron, which in Froese's and Baumann's hands were to become emblematic of the band's output over much of the 1970s. As the final release on the Ohr record label, *Atem* was a suitably impressive conclusion to the group's formative years.

There were also significant concerts during the year – one in Switzerland, four in Germany and eight in France, of which those at Les Ponts-de-Cé Open Air Festival and Alhambra Theatre Saint-Ouen are the best-known. At four gigs – including La Rochelle Roanne Troyes in Paris on August 24, and 27 August in Ratingen, Germany – none other than Klaus Schulze played along. There are no known recordings of these concerts, though photographs do exist.

In the summer, Baumann went off travelling through India and Nepal. Froese and Franke – knowing their time at Ohr was over, yet not knowing where next to turn – spent some time in Berlin's Skyline Studios making recordings that they hoped would speak on their behalf. These recordings became the album *Green Desert*, but they were never released at the time (see Chapter 12), since with Baumann returning to Europe and new hope on the horizon, there were other paths to follow.

Green Desert (1986)

Personnel:
Edgar Froese: organ, guitar, keyboards
Chris Franke: drums, percussion, organ, keyboards
Producer: Tangerine Dream
Recorded at Skyline Studios, Berlin: August 1973
Release date: January 1986
Chart placings: -
Running time: 38:22
All tracks by Froese, Franke
Side One: 1. 'Green Desert'
Side Two: 1. 'White Clouds' 2. 'Astral Traveller' 3. 'Indian Summer'

Green Desert – recorded in the summer between the end of Ohr and the beginning of Virgin – was intended to be an indication of what Froese and Franke could achieve and wished to do in the studio. It featured organ, keyboards – including a new Minimoog – guitar and drums. Franke had a brand new rhythm controller from an Italian manufacturer, which he was impressed with, both in its appearance and utility. (This was the EKO ComputeRhythm, also used by Jean-Michel Jarre to great effect on his first two albums. Manuel Göttsching of Ashra was a devotee too.) In due course, he used it to trigger sequences from other synths, making it the first recorded use of this sequencing setup.

The opening title track begins with an ominous drone, its cutoff frequency slowly raised then lowered. Eerie synth whistles follow as the drone continues to rise and fall, until a reverberated chord and other effects enter, adding colour to the sparse opening textures. Some of these sounds seem to be VCS3-generated, some are other keyboards. The effect is of some faraway nation, its spectral music transmitted over radio (Froese commented much later that Tangerine Dream music was travel music, often inspired by the landscapes and countries he saw). After a few minutes, Franke makes some cymbal splashes as other sounds emerge: some light, some a little more ominous. Now there is a hint of industrial complexes in the metallic timbres of certain sounds, though still the bass drone anchors it all.

After a couple more minutes, Franke sets up a drum pattern, beginning with snare and kick drum before heading off to the tom toms. The effect of this drumming with the keyboard bass is particularly suspenseful, the tension increasing as Froese's guitar solo begins. Slowly, the piece develops, the drums increasing in complexity, new keyboard sounds adding texture, while Froese's guitar solo progresses. By the time we are ten minutes into the piece, the music has unfurled still further, with the drums reaching maximum effect and complexity: a wonderfully atmospheric opening section. As the drums come to their awesome cymbal-crashing, tom-beating climax, the piece subsides into a wash of keyboard chords and sustained notes. Alas, this album was the last time Franke drummed on any recorded Tangerine Dream music.

The track's conclusion drifts into keyboard sounds and chords, notably a string synth. After a few minutes – once a melodic coda has played out – the ambient section also subsides. This piece alone would have intrigued any record label. As it was, when Richard Branson at Virgin heard it, he was motivated to consider Tangerine Dream's new music along with their Ohr catalogue for imported LP sales.

Side B opens with 'White Clouds' and more of Franke's drum work, to which string synths and other keyboards are added. A second melodic theme carries this piece, itself doubled with a harmony section. The feel is light, almost airy: positive, sunny. Now the drums do not suggest threat; more a sense of motion. The listener might be travelling in a high-speed train in some exotic location. This piece is only five minutes long, however – a short trip – ending in another keyboard drone and a few synth effects, some of which sound like birdsong.

'Astral Voyager' opens with a high-energy sequence, to which keyboard chords and held notes are added. The sequence changes key but not timbre as the piece develops. This template would be used to great effect over the coming years as the group developed their trademark Berlin School sound. Slowly, more melodic elements enter the mix, notably a high-register keyboard playing a fluttering solo. Again, this sounds like a piece describing motion, but this time it must be through some imaginary astral plane – nothing terrestrial. The effect is light and fleet-footed. As the solo continues, so does the journey, until – as the piece comes to its conclusion – the timbre of the sequence does change, alerting the listener to the terminus, which is evoked in a wash of keyboards.

The concluding piece 'Indian Summer' begins with string-synth chords and a few synth effects. These chords repeat into a cycling pattern as white noise washes over the listener. The feel is sombre, perhaps melancholic, as if mourning for summers lost in the past. After a while, a harmonising bass enters, and more string synth, elaborating the composition into something more substantial; then another fluttering high-register synth takes up a solo. This mood continues for a few minutes, with some variation in timbre and arrangement. Here, the phased-chord backing is particularly noteworthy: the pair had a new phaser to use. Soon afterwards, an undistorted volume-pedal guitar solo takes up the lead position, under which more white noise effects swirl. This is definitely a melancholy mood: autumn is close.

At length, the music loses its rhythmic structure and descends into a wash of string-synth chords, the guitar solo's closing part and more white noise effects. At its conclusion, it fades into silence. Autumn is here.

This album, while not quite in the same league as *Atem*, *Phaedra* or *Rubycon*, nevertheless stands up well to those classics. The latter three tracks do not have the same musical development and sense of progression as other works, but each is strong in its own right for all that the overall feel is somewhat static. But these three tracks all have their own charm, and even beauty, while 'Astral Voyager' is notable for its early use of a sequencer.

It was in Britain, though, that the next phase of the group would occur. With John Peel playing *Atem* regularly on his show and singing its praises, British fans – already with their ears open to the new progressive sounds of Yes, Pink Floyd, King Crimson and many more – realised that in Tangerine Dream something unique and well worth their attention had appeared. This strong, vibrant underground scene was, however, beginning to acquire commercial success too, as the world-striding *The Dark Side Of The Moon* would illustrate. Record labels were on the lookout for suitable groups to add to their roster. Just a year or two had passed since the first offerings of the British progressive scene, led in the main by Yes and Pink Floyd, but now groups from other nations – not least West Germany: Can, Popol Vuh, Neu! – were appearing, their music enjoyed by many a British music fan. Thus it was that the unlikely name of Tangerine Dream became known in Britain.

Among the many people who heard that name in 1973 was a youthful, self-confident entrepreneur named Richard Branson. Branson's fledgling business specialised in importing LPs from the continent, selling upwards of 15,000 Tangerine Dream albums on the strength of Peel's repeated paeans to the group. But Branson had already had his first stroke of luck. A tape of an extraordinary 25-minute piece of music called 'Opus One' (soon to be retitled 'Tubular Bells') had come his way the previous year via his music production team of Simon Heyworth and Tom Newman, leading him to prepare for Mike Oldfield's debut. He was on the lookout for more, and Tangerine Dream seemed perfect.

By summer, Froese and his group were in London, talking with Branson about a record deal. Accounts vary as to how this negotiation progressed. At this stage, Virgin Records was hardly known, *Tubular Bells* having only been released a few months earlier and selling slowly (the use of its music for the film *The Exorcist* would bring global attention at the end of the year, allowing Virgin Records to expand). Branson and Nik Powell had begun their music business as Virgin Records and Tapes – a small shop in Notting Hill Gate – and this is where the German trio arrived. Legend has it that Froese and Branson negotiated the main points of the five-year deal on the shop's wooden steps, with Branson playing Froese a cassette tape of *Tubular Bells* afterwards. However it went, we now know that history was being made.

In their interview in issue 14 of *Prog m*agazine, Froese and Franke recalled those summer days. The initial meetings included chess on Branson's houseboat moored on the Thames. Froese recalled: 'He lost three and won two against me'. According to Baumann, they were 'chasing girls and playing tennis at (Branson's) house. It was hot, so we'd just play in our underwear'. Froese and Branson signed the actual contract in early September 1973. A charming photograph exists showing the pair outside a branch of Thresher's wine merchants; Branson playing up to the camera, Froese resplendent in dark trousers, shirt and a tan-coloured jacket, more dignified.

As the year faded into autumn, the trio were booked into Branson's Manor Studio. Branson owned the Manor house at Shipton-on-Cherwell in Oxfordshire, where Heyworth and Newman were at the head of his music production team. At this stage, only a few albums had been recorded in the studio there, including classics by The Bonzo Dog Band, Magma, Gong, John Cale and Sandy Denny. But Tangerine Dream were not the first German musicians to enjoy the facilities: Faust recorded *Faust IV* there in June of that year. On November 20, Tangerine Dream arrived at the Manor to begin what would be momentous recordings.

Baumann recalled the mood of the recording sessions in his 2020 interview with *musicradar.com*:

> From day one, everything was improvised. Then, we would go back and maybe add some strange noises – this is before the synths. We would

> run around the studio looking for things we could hit or smash. We'd hit piano strings or scratch them. Anything that would give us a new sound ... For a while, we started recording (these sounds) on a two-track tape, and when we needed a particular sound, we'd find that bit of tape and press play. If we missed the cue, we had to do it again. Sometimes we'd turn the tape over and play it backwards. It was all very random and quite chaotic ... it was the prehistoric age!

In the same interview, Baumann also recalled the logistics of using huge pieces of musical equipment:

> Actually getting us into the Manor Studio in Oxfordshire – where we recorded *Phaedra* – was a big job. A truck would gather our equipment in Berlin, then take the road and the ferry. It took maybe half a day to set up the equipment, but we never hurried. It was a very relaxed atmosphere ... probably thanks to the hash!

By now – albeit in sluggish and frustrating style – new music was beginning to take shape, and it sounded unlike anything heard before. With Branson's advance in their pockets, Froese and the group had purchased a Moog synthesizer and sequencer, knowing it would be the key to their future musical development. In an interview given to Mark Prendergast for the 1994 Virgin Records box set of *Tangents*, Froese recalled those legendary recording sessions:

> We worked each day from eleven o'clock in the morning to two o'clock at night. By the eleventh day, we barely had six and a half minutes of music on tape. Technically, everything that could go wrong did go wrong. The tape machine broke down, there were repeated mixing console failures, and the speakers were damaged because of the unusually low frequencies of the bass notes ... Fortunately, after a two-day break in the countryside, a new start brought a breakthrough: 'Mysterious Semblance At The Strand Of Nightmares' was recorded on 4th December. Peter and Chris were asleep after a long recording session, so I invited my wife, Monique, into the studio. I called in the studio engineer and recorded it in one take on a double-keyboard Mellotron while Monique turned the knobs on the phasing device. The piece is on the record exactly as it was recorded that day. And this practice was due to continue for the rest of the session ... On the title track, Chris pressed the button to start

> the bubbling bass note. Unfortunately, the bass pattern didn't work the way it should have – after a few seconds, as you can hear on the album, the note drops in but out of tune. Chris then started tuning the bass sequence while running it. What he didn't know, was that I had told the engineer to press the recording button whenever music or some sounds could be heard. So what you hear in the beginning of 'Phaedra' is a rehearsal! Even when I started playing the melody line, it was just a try – no one thought it would go on the record.

Technical problems continued. With a three-week deadline, the task was difficult. These early analogue synthesizers used voltage-controlled oscillators, which meant their operation was susceptible to change according to variations in room temperature. Just preparing the instruments took hours. In addition, the machines had no facility for recalling previous settings, except for turning knobs, dials and sliders to the same positions – but that did not mean the same sound necessarily emerged.

It was only in 2019 that fans of the group were able to hear some of the unused music recorded in these sessions. In the 18-disc collection *In Search Of Hades*, there are two CDs of outtakes – music by turns extraordinary, fascinating and moving (for instance, Baumann's unused recorder-playing). It is an essential purchase for all fans.

The group continued to use their improvisatory compositional method. In his 2020 interview with Danny Scott at *musicradar.com*, Baumann recalled it:

> Even when we added sequencers, we used to play them live. The ones that we used, allowed you to skip notes and steps as you went along, so they became another one of our live instruments ... There was no preparation (for *Phaedra*). Nothing at all. We just switched on the synths, smoked a joint and made some noise. In fact, *Phaedra* specifically ... I can remember we did that whole first section in one go. We worked on it afterwards of course. We'd listen back and start treating different sections of the music. We used a lot of tape loops, plus the outboard gear, like flangers ... wah-wah pedals and different delays. Yes, a lot of work went into the album, but the original music was all improvised. Maybe one overdub, I think: the flute part.

Improvisation allowed the trio to experience their music as it really was. In the same interview, Baumann recalled their reactions: 'There was really never a *wrong* note, just parts that didn't fit as well. But that was not a reason to stop playing ... as long as it didn't throw the mood of the track. In the studio, we would keep recording and edit out anything that went against the grain'.

Froese, too, was aware of the trailblazing scope of their work. In the *Prog* magazine interview, he recalled programming and using synthesizers:

> It goes back to my early years as a pupil of classical music, when I realised that everything in musical structure is bass-oriented. We were the first band to ever use the Moog Modular system as a stand-alone sequencer. The programming of those sequences was time-consuming, but it gave the endless freedom to improvise on top of those bass lines. Without exaggerating our musical capabilities, we were very much ahead of our time.

In his 1986 interview with *Totally Wired,* Froese recalled their approach to electronic instruments:

> People who associate us with electronic music have possibly forgotten that the hardware was just a bridge to reach our musical goals. I still think that even without all that stuff, we are still able to use our imagination and follow our fantasies; if you lose your imagination, then you cannot create anything, even if you've got the most expensive computer in the world.

Franke had a similar view in the same interview:

> Electronics were just one possible way to go. If some genius had created a better Mellotron, maybe we'd just use acoustic bits and pieces. We didn't have to have the electronic synthesizer to create that style; the idea was there and then we looked for the instruments ... We were in the position that we didn't have anyone to copy. We started from scratch.

Froese had by now begun using an instrument which he found irresistible: the Mellotron. First used in recordings of note by The Beatles at Abbey Road, it was a very early kind of sampler, in that pre-recorded loops of sound created by real instruments could be played back by pressing the appropriate key. Mellotrons had a unique, instantly recognisable palette of sounds and were used to great effect by other bands, notably King Crimson – who favoured the strings loops – and Genesis. Klaus Schulze later went on to make spectacular use of the choir recordings. For Froese and Baumann, however, it was the flute sounds which attracted them most.

Little did Froese realise what effect he and his bandmates' devotion to their art would have on the British public in particular. Tangerine Dream's halcyon days lay just ahead.

1974 – Success, Moog, Gigs

The title of their forthcoming first Virgin Records album came from Greek myth. In his interview with Johnny Black for issue 17 of *ThisBEAT* in April 1986, Froese explained the reference: 'We've always been interested in Greek mythology, and the titles on this album come from there. Not just Greek, but Egyptian, Indian, European – philosophy mixed with a bit of humour.'

Phaedra (1974)

Personnel:
Edgar Froese: mellotron, guitar, bass, VCS3 synthesizer, organ
Chris Franke: Moog synthesizer, VCS3 synthesizer
Peter Baumann: organ, electric piano, VCS3 synthesizer, flute
Producer: Tangerine Dream
Recorded at the Manor, Oxfordshire: November 1973
Release date: UK and US: February 1974
Chart placings: UK: 15
Running time: 37:33
Side One: 1. 'Phaedra' (Froese, Franke, Baumann)
Side Two: 1. 'Mysterious Semblance At The Strand Of Nightmares' (Froese) 2. 'Movements Of A Visionary' (Froese, Franke, Baumann) 3. 'Sequent C' (Baumann)

The album's side-long title track opens with strangely oscillating sounds like bells bent into resonant spheres and struck by soft beaters. We are in deep space; only stars visible. As more metallic sounds chime in the background – all of them deeply reverberated – the sounds mutate into bubbling sequences, bleeping and warbling. When the tempo slows, a delay comes in, lending the sequences structure and regularity, albeit still accompanied by odd sounds; the time signature is now four-to-the-bar. Synths clang as if from the end of a great hall, and the overall mood is icy, distant – no sign of warmth.

As the key changes, the weird effects continue, before underlying Mellotron choir chords anchor the sequence so that it has a complete structure. Now the Mellotron choir is dark, accompanied by keyboard chords, until massively-phased Mellotron strings come in, playing just two chords, then a couple more, varying the accompaniment until it transforms into a non-repeating ascending line.

Without warning, the mood changes. A quick delay transforms a plucked sound into something resembling a guitar. More clinking, clattering synths follow this part, before the sequence returns, along with further Mellotron chords. Now the sequence is fast and simple, just three notes with a slight delay: sometimes unaccompanied, sometimes with extra oscillators. The phased sounds are deep, the oscillating accompaniment like the messages of alien spacecraft.

In 4/4 time, the sequence transforms again, now accompanied by guitar and new synth sounds, until a menacing keyboard playing a bass note brings a new mood. The sequences change key, though the bass note remains, giving the listener a sense of eerie vertigo; now more sounds come in as the sequencer pitch rises then settles in one key. The sensation of headlong motion is intense: flight, pursuit or something worse.

Again and again, the key changes, now denuded of accompaniment, until, as if unable to stop, it reaches a high pitch, then – in deep delay – oscillates in ever-shorter time signatures, then halting, taken away by delay and deep reverberation.

Nothing is left except for weird bleeps and cosmic effects. The sonic space is almost empty now, and the listener is lost – lacking reference points, floating, spinning, alone. But after a minute, a new sound emerges, as if from some rescuing alien. Yet the listener is unable to understand the language; this curious, almost whimsical repeated phrase just hangs in audio space – mutating, changing, yet always enigmatic. To counterpoint it, choral sounds drift in and out, and then the alien voice departs.

Now all that is left is space – a choral drift, the Mellotron choir, underpinned by a deeper keyboard hinting at the fundamental structure of the universe. As another alien voice briefly sounds, an organ line takes us through the cosmos, accompanied by more Mellotron strings. Serene chords underpin a rising Mellotron line, as if echoing the revealed grandeur of the universe, depicted for the listener with ever-more detail.

This piece evokes space, yet also manages to describe a journey through it. Beloved of most fans, it remains one of the great explorations of space music.

The B-side is split into three pieces, the opening one being 'Mysterious Semblance At The Strand Of Nightmares', which begins with dense phased Mellotron strings chords vying with white noise. As more spacey sounds enter the mix, the tension increases through subtle chord changes, until –

as the phasing deepens still further – a gothic atmosphere is created, like the theme tune of some Teutonic forest monster.

Suddenly, halfway through, rhythm is added to the Mellotron: a kind of quickstep march, accompanied by new chords. It is as if whatever gothic entity was approaching is now passing by. Then the chords change again, the rhythm fades, and more phasing transforms the piece: every sound this time. As weird accompanying synths begin to arrive, the original chords return, phased as before, with bubbling synths and occasional bleeps, until, eventually, rolling white noise winds take over the piece, wresting control from the Mellotron before it returns to dominance – and with it, a chattering VCS3 sound.

The second track on side B – 'Movements Of A Visionary' – opens with sounds like the hissing voice of a space prophet: Baumann's voice being processed through a VCS3 synth, given style and movement through the use of reverberation and echo units. To this opening, a whirring synth is added: the alien reply to human speech perhaps. After a while, a rippling sequence in 3/4 time emerges in the higher registers, given form and motion by an echo unit. VCS3 chatter accompanies this oscillating ostinato, with the return of white noise also. Under this spacey melange, an organ brings something more mysterious: density of structure, its simple chords whirring.

As Fender Rhodes and synth notes begin to bubble up, the piece acquires something lighter in tone, moving on from its enigmatic opening, with the sequence, basically unaltered, now offering hope in the darkness. As the piece develops, these two themes oppose one another – sometimes dense, even dark, at other times, especially via the organ, lighter, almost translucent. This organ recalls past pieces from the early 1970s, especially when the sequence moves from 3/4 time to 2/4. In due course, the sequences begin to vary more, changing register and rhythm – in part through control of the synthesizer, in part through changing the delay – and towards the conclusion of the piece, the variation is considerable, using notes out of standard scales before returning to a formal structure. At the piece's end, the alien synth sound returns, then the music fades away.

The final track on side B is Baumann's piece 'Sequent C', edited to fit on the LP, which opens with him playing a treble recorder multitracked four times through an echo unit. The mood is mournful – these are the drawn-out notes of a melancholy creature, given life through music in a minor key. Delay units and reverberation accentuate the glissando on some notes as the piece develops, but essentially this is a two-minute window into some solemn ritual: left simple, sad, but whole. It's an affecting conclusion to the album, which seems to mostly evoke space and the structure of the universe, yet which, at its end, does not forget the human experience of such environments.

Many Tangerine Dream fans regard *Phaedra* as the band's best and most important work. What was unexpected, however, was the commercial and critical response. Thanks to John Peel's enthusiastic and continuing support of the band (none of the group gave press interviews), *Phaedra* managed to break the UK top-20 album chart, peaking at number fifteen. Released on 20 February, it remained on that chart for an amazing fifteen weeks. This commercial success greatly cheered both band and label.

The critical response varied, albeit mostly positive. Yet there were naysayers. Once the album had entered *Melody Maker*'s charts and risen even higher than in the national charts – to number 9 – a reviewer cast his eyes and ears over the release. That reviewer was Steve Lake, and he wrote, 'As far as I'm concerned, *Phaedra* is gutless and spineless, devoid of inspiration, imagination or plain old-fashioned funk. But maybe a few hundred thousand potential record buyers can't be wrong'. He continued by calling Froese 'a failed heavy guitarist'. In their interview for *Prog* magazine issue 14, Froese recalled that response.

> We didn't have a great open-minded crowd in our early days. There was a rejection attitude all the way through till we reached number 10 with *Phaedra* on the *Melody Maker* charts. I remember the first-ever LP review in Britain was half a page in *Melody Maker*. Steve Lake opened the review with the headline, 'Eat more shit – 100,000 flies can't be wrong'. But that was our breakthrough into the international market, even if Lake would have done everything to protect the market from the 'German knob-turners'. He hated us.

Baumann recalled Lake's review in the same interview: 'I remember that '100,000 flies' line well. When Virgin picked up *Phaedra,* we had chart success. But there were obviously still a lot of people saying, 'What the hell is that?'.

Upon the release of *In Search Of Hades* in 2019, fans heard some of the unused music from those magical sessions for the first time. Two discs of music never before released from the *Phaedra* recordings were part of the box set, and they were fascinating.

Phaedra Out-takes Volume 1

Personnel:
Edgar Froese: mellotron, guitar, bass, VCS3 synthesizer, organ
Chris Franke: Moog synthesizer, VCS3 synthesizer
Peter Baumann: organ, electric piano, VCS3 synthesizer, flute
Producer: Tangerine Dream
Recorded at the Manor, Oxfordshire: November 1973
Release date: UK and US: October 2019
Chart placings: -
Running time: 52:12
All tracks by Froese, Franke, Baumann
Tracks: 1. 'Second Day' 2. 'Flute Organ Piece' 3. 'Phaedra Out-take Version 2A'

The opening track begins with sparse, shimmering notes and a few reverberated sound effects. The mood is cool, even cold. As the shimmering keyboard reaches out and begins harmonising with itself, a sonic effect like the first hints of dawn begins, with the higher notes sounding like the last rain of the night. Mellotron chords come in – a stronger, deeper timbre to anchor the shimmering notes – until, after a while, this instrument is the main sound; then it fades, so that the two main keyboard sounds float around each other, occasionally changing key, mostly in the same key. With new tinkling notes in a high register, it is clear that all three musicians are contributing to the improvisation. After five minutes, a deep phasing effect is added to the Mellotron, but this fades as new sound effects enter the mix – VCS3 chatter, mostly, with other effects hardly audible – until a looped sequence emerges. This sequence soon takes over, though the Mellotron can still be heard. It is like the sudden firing of a spacecraft engine, which rises in pitch as the music intensifies: launch imminent. As the reverberation applied to the foreground instruments changes, the sequence alters pitch again so that it seems to be an aerial entity – a mechanical creature perhaps, looping, rising and falling, looking down on the staid environment the Mellotron and other keyboards portray. It is a fantastic arrangement, guaranteed to evoke flight, space, aerial motion.

Halfway through the piece, the Mellotron fades and the sequence is muted, leaving, once again, the shimmering keyboard. Now, alien birdsong sounds enter the mix, and the Mellotron takes an upward flight, abandoning all key and formal structure, rising ever higher until it fades. All that remains now are the sequences and strange water sounds, as if indicating the final status of the spacecraft, which then departs anyway.

That spacecraft is replaced by a more traditional Tangerine Dream sequence in 8/4 time: deep, delayed, oscillating. Above and around it, the Mellotron swirls – phased again, as if twisting in its dance around the sequence. A high-register metallic keyboard adds other colours to the mix. With the sequences increasing in intensity and rising in pitch, the other keyboards add occasional notes but seem lost, as if the Moog is taking over. After a while, another Mellotron arrives – smoother strings – to accompany the sequence, which then, almost at once, makes a dramatic, melancholy drop to much deeper notes. Now the sequences are changing every few seconds; then they flatten to one note and return again, taking the lead, then collapsing, cycling, fading and losing their delay. All the listener can hear now is the original keyboard, swirling half-drunk Mellotron chords, and a last echo of the sequences, which are almost unrecognisable. As the sequences fade, all that is left are the first two keyboards playing around the root note. This piece did not reach the released album, but at just over twenty minutes it seems likely to have been envisaged as one side of an LP.

At first, the second piece revolves around Baumann's deeply-mournful flute, which, with reverb and delay, becomes a fabulously melancholy, wordless voice. Against this, a solemn organ plays, but it is muted, as if played in elegy. With the arrival of a subtle ostinato, the piece opens out a little, until the whole spectrum is filled with organ tones: some a drone, others hopping and fluttering far above. A delayed keyboard (a little like an electric guitar) adds extra texture. As the root note drops, a tone then returns, the piece opening out still further, with the addition of more shimmering Rhodes keyboard notes – and this is the form for a while. As the organ ostinato develops into something resembling some of Terry Riley's early work, the piece begins to move – not in any direction, but in and out, like some strange sonic sea creature alive in the depths with flashing lights. At length, the various strands come together into a beautiful ever-mutating chord: part-drone, part-loops, part-fluttering-solo-notes. It is amazing to think that well over forty years passed by before the group's fans could hear this lovely piece: the highlight of this disc for certain.

The third track is another twenty-minute piece, which can be regarded as an embryonic version of 'Mysterious Semblance At The Strand Of Nightmares' – some days later Froese decided to play the melody on the Mellotron instead of the piano. Opening with metallic percussion and muted piano notes, it sounds more like early Glastonbury ambience than anything – very nice! As the piano part mutates and progresses accompanied by the bells and gong, the listener is suddenly reminded of the famous piano piece from *Encore*: at least, its opening phrases. Then a filtered note enters the mix, soon to dominate it, accompanied only by wisps of synth and a few metallic tinkles. In due course, however, Mellotron strings arrive, bringing a more stately feel to the music, as with the first piece. The drone note remains constant, anchoring the improvisation until all elements are in unison. At this point, a rhythmic bass sound begins, giving the piece forward momentum, beautifully accompanied by woozy synth notes that almost match, but, brilliantly, don't quite. Now the Mellotron takes the lead, deeply-phased, as so often (the same effect fascinated Klaus Schulze in his 1973 recordings), and full of pomp and ceremony. There are hints of the sound worlds of *Zeit* in this section, evoked by that peculiar rhythmic thrust and the semi-random synth flutterings oscillating around it.

Eventually, however, the Mellotron departs, leaving a keyboard sound like an anguished voice, around which white noise blasts detonate, all accompanied by the deeper, harsher rhythmic propulsion which by now has acquired a high resonance and a distinct delay. When the Mellotron returns, it seems as though some vast, complex, majestic procession is being evoked: noble and suffused in ancient ceremony. As the VCS3 chatter acquires a voice-like quality, the Mellotron theme fades, just one riff now, as if to mark the arrival of a new participant. And then the brilliant conclusion: a *real* voice can be heard – crazed, perhaps mad, uttering vocalisations to match the underlying music's intensity. It is an extraordinary moment, with vocal sounds that – as photographs of live concerts at the time prove – were made either by Baumann or Franke.

The piece's last few minutes drift into white noise and more vocal utterances, supported by the Mellotron and a constant VCS3 burble. The end of the procession has arrived. The participants, including the main one, have departed. All that remains is their sonic debris – ready to be cleaned up by the liberal use of reverberation and delay, and topped off by the brief return of the piano and metallic percussion.

While none of these pieces suits the *Phaedra* LP known and loved by fans, that is known only in hindsight. Musically, all three are the equal of what Virgin Records released in this momentous year for the group. A marvellous trip, essential for all fans.

Phaedra Out-takes Volume 2

Personnel:
Edgar Froese: mellotron, guitar, bass, VCS3 synthesizer, organ
Chris Franke: Moog synthesizer, VCS3 synthesizer
Peter Baumann: organ, electric piano, VCS3 synthesizer, flute
Producer: Tangerine Dreams
Recorded at the Manor, Oxfordshire: November 1973
Release date: UK and US: October 2019
Chart placings: -
Running time: 45:45
All tracks by Froese, Franke, Baumann
Tracks: 1. 'Phaedra Out-take 1' 2. 'Phaedra Out-take 2B' 3. '2nd Side Piece 1' 4. '2nd Side Piece 2' 5. 'Organ piece'

The first outtake of the second disc begins with a haunting synth note and some deep, dense, doomy Mellotron chords, which slowly fill out, then play alone. Soon, a more brassy keyboard enters the mix, harmonising with the drone but also matching the Mellotron. This section recalls opening parts of classic live concerts of the time – all three elements working in harmony, all three composed of chords or lines. After five minutes, however, the mood changes, becoming more uncertain with a hint of tension beneath it, until one of the keyboards acquires a glassy tone and begins a two-note loop. This motif then fades, but is replaced by even heavier Mellotron chords. At the piece's conclusion, the mood is perhaps more elegiac than doomy, in the main due to more excellent use of a shimmering Rhodes sound and a lovely two-chord progression.

The second piece, 'Out-take 2B', opens with a frenetic Moog sequence, leaping around in all directions as if out of control, below which various held notes and chords play. That the sequence is not delayed gives it a much more immediate, forceful presence in the mix. At length, the much-used phased Mellotron strings arrive, until a minute or so later, when the sequence mutes and the Mellotron fades. Tension springs up. The volume is low, the frequencies bassy. Then a delay unit kicks in, and suddenly the listener is ascending, conveyed by delay, reverberation and a few spectral Mellotron strings chords into the skies. When those elements are gone, a cycling sequence arrives, looped in no particular key, but chasing itself up and down the scales; soon accompanied by filtered white noise and a throbbing drone. But at length, at the end of this brief outtake, all that is left is much reverb and a mournful Mellotron playing the 'Mysterious Semblance' riff from 'Out-take 2A'.

The third piece returns the listener to the world of the piano, with its metallic percussion accompaniment. A drone supports these various elements, which again have a curiously New Age feel to them (perhaps evoked by the association of temple bells with hippie culture). As the piano part begins to develop, the drone deepens, bringing a certain solemnity but also a sense of anticipation, enhanced by the piano's staccato feel and some accompanying synth lines. It is rather strange to hear the melodic element here, as it so precisely evokes Klaus Schulze's use of one-tone drops, but that mood soon departs, to be replaced by whirling, drifting Mellotron strings once again. In due course, a rhythmic element emerges: a pulsing chord that rises and falls through volume and filtering. This sound also has a curiously mid-period Schulze-esque feel to it, which is odd to hear in so early a piece! But in due course, the Mellotron opens out and begins to dominate, now accompanied by a Rhodes piano. At length, however, what remains is a high-pitched pulse and the mesmeric cycling Mellotron, so that the listener is brought back to reality in gentle fashion.

Piece four is another short track: just nine minutes long. It opens as if in an airport, with footsteps and reverberated voices, beneath which bassy thumps rumble. Soon though, a metallic piano sound scatters itself over the ambience, each note a seed, with a whirring keyboard underneath it. As the seeds become denser chords, this second keyboard also acquires depth and reverberation, so that soon the listener seems to be inside some bizarre glasshouse full of musical plants. Some of these plants are dangerous: we know that from the atonal chords and dark, scything synth tones. Then, more mechanical elements arrive: VCS3 chatter and burble, and another of Franke's looped sequences, which has no particular frame of reference, but which cycles – oscillating, changing, floating above the main thrust of the music, as if it is an avian recorder of the greenery below. Still, the piano chords strike: danger remains. As new reverberated sounds arrive – distant applause or distant machines – the sequence takes on a regular form and begins to disappear into reverberation. Then a new keyboard solo begins, high and haunting, around which white noise and voices hiss and splutter. It is tremendously evocative – of enigmatic machinery, of great transparent environments, of unknowable creatures flying just out of reach. Perhaps

Above: Peter Baumann, Chris Franke and Edgar Froese in 1976.

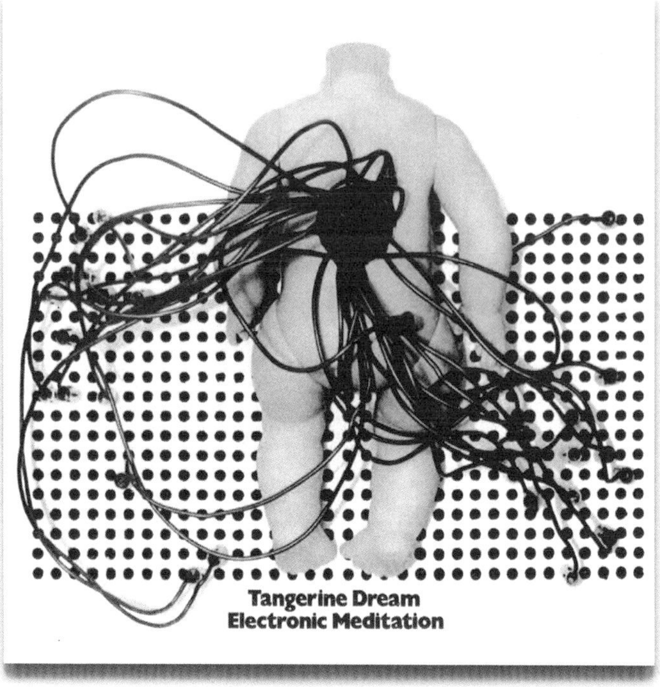

Left: The *Electronic Meditation* album cover in the standard Ohr Records style, created by Reinhard Hippen. (*Ohr Records*)

Right: *Alpha Centauri* album cover using a painting by Edgar Froese. (*Ohr Records*)

Right: The *Zeit* album cover was another painting by Edgar Froese. (*Ohr Records*)

Left: A third painting by Edgar Froese (featuring his son Jerome) adorned the *Atem* LP cover. (*Ohr Records*)

Left: Franke, Froese and Baumann in an early Virgin Records promotional photograph. (*Virgin Records*)

Right: Froese, Franke and Baumann at the filmed Coventry Cathedral concert in 1975.

Left: Another early Virgin promo photograph of Froese, Baumann and Franke. (*Virgin Records*)

Right: A photographic portrait of Edgar Froese. (*photo courtesy David Elliott*)

Left: Chris Franke in the studio. (*photo courtesy David Elliott*)

Right: An arty shot of Peter Baumann looking out over New York. (*photo courtesy David Elliott*)

Left: The on-body artwork for the CD of *Green Desert,* recorded in 1973 but not released until 1986. (*Jive Electro*)

Right: The cover for the band's 1974 masterpiece *Phaedra* was created by Edgar Froese. (*Virgin Records*)

Right: Advert artwork for the 1974 Tangerine Dream British tour. (*scan courtesy Steve Jones*)

Left: A Japanese advert for the Ohr Records back catalogue.

Left: Edgar Froese playing at the Coventry Cathedral concert of 4 October 1975.

Right: Chris Franke and the Big Moog at Coventry Cathedral in 1975.

Left: The Coventry Cathedral concert of 1975. This long shot shows how the band's set-up contrasted with the cathedral's interiors. Designed by Basil Spence, it had only been consecrated in 1962 – just 13 years prior to this concert.

Right: Peter Baumann concentrates at Coventry Catherdral.

Left: Another shot of Chris Franke playing the Big Moog at Coventry Cathedral.

Right: Froese and Franke concentrate hard at Coventry Cathedral.

Left: Chris Franke at Coventry Cathedral.

Right: Peter Baumann and the EMS VCS3 synthesizer.

Left: A final shot from Coventry Cathedral, featuring Peter Baumann.

Right: Edgar Froese playing his Fender Stratocaster on German TV in 1976.

Left: Peter Baumann is surrounded by keyboards in this improvised performance from German TV.

Right: Chris Franke works the Big Moog from the same performance.

Left: *Oedipus Tyrannus* was a play adapted by Keith Mitchell staged at the Chichester Festival – music by Tangerine Dream. (*Virgin Records*)

Right: The *Rubycon* LP cover was a photograph taken by Monique Froese. (Virgin Records)

Right: *Ricochet* was adorned by a photograph taken by Monique Froese at the Bordeaux seaside. (*Virgin Records*)

Left: The LP cover for *Sorcerer* was a dramatic still image taken from the film. (*MCA*)

Left: The *Stratosfear* album cover used another photograph taken by Monique Froese. (*Virgin Records*)

Right: *Encore* used a photograph of the group playing on their successful US tour in 1977. (*Virgin Records*)

Right: The *Cyclone* LP had a beautiful and enigmatic painting by Edgar Froese. (*Virgin Records*)

Left: For *Force Majeure,* the painting and design work was done by Monique Froese. (*Virgin Records*)

Left and below: The 2019 *In Search of Hades* box set includes many wonderful bonuses, including the Victoria Palace Theatre and Rainbow concerts from 1974. It has an excellent essay by Tangerine Dream archivist Wouter Bessels and new mixes of *Phaedra* and *Ricochet* by Steven Wilson. (*Virgin Records*)

this is our world; perhaps another. We cannot know. The organ solo will not tell us – only suggest. This piece is certainly the highlight of the second disc, a marvellous, albeit short demonstration of the group's range, insight and technical mastery so early in their career.

The final track is a brief organ piece, opening with a chord which drifts in sparse, chilled fashion into the upper regions of our atmosphere, and probably thence into space. It evokes ascent, though not powered; this is more of a slow float into the sky. String synths are our weather, rippling keyboard motifs our clouds. Everything is blue and tranquil, warmed by the sun, which is that original organ chord. Even when the listener is buffeted by sequences and brief atonal key alterations, the music rises on, ascending on a single chord with nothing to halt its progress. This is a marvellously evocative piece describing either physical or mental ascent into regions mysterious.

As with the first disc of outtakes, this music shows the range of the group's vision and their willingness to explore entirely new regions of sound and composition. Although this is the music of the cutting-room floor, these are glorious pieces that did not make the final LP because they were essentially work in progress. Although there was no room for them, they are all wonderful in their own right.

Once *Phaedra*'s success was apparent, everyone turned their thoughts to concerts. What followed during that year and the subsequent one was a series of gigs – mostly in Britain – beloved of fans of the trio for their improvised style, their reach and depth, and for the sheer, amazing, exciting wonder of experiencing the group; sometimes playing in halls, sometimes at more impressive venues, such as the cathedrals of late 1974 and 1975. But in 1974, there were 23 gigs at British venues, with just one in Germany and one in France. These gigs have gone down in legend, recorded and restored in the epic Tangerine Tree project – a network of fans releasing the best recordings of the concerts on a not-for-profit basis. Two of the best-known concerts are London's Victoria Palace Theatre gig of 16 June (the group's British live debut), and the London Rainbow concert of 26 October: both recorded by the Manor mobile studio.

Live At The Victoria Palace Theatre, London

Personnel:

Edgar Froese: Mellotron, VCS3 synthesizer

Chris Franke: Moog synthesizer, keyboards, VCS3 synthesizer

Peter Baumann: organ, electric piano, VCS3 synthesizer
Recorded by the Manor Mobile: 16th June 1974
Mixer: Phil Newell
Release date: UK and US: October 2019
Chart placings: -
Running time: 88:11 (Two discs)
All tracks by Froese, Franke, Baumann
Tracks: 1. 'Part 1' 2. 'Part 2' 3. 'Encore'

The concert opens with a delicate, drifting chord that, after a few moments, becomes more of a drone, then a two-note chord, with both notes set against one another. As the drone acquires a bass section – also drifting between the two ominous notes – the whole piece begins to gather new forms to itself, often with heavy vibrato, mostly keeping to the root note, sometimes adding a harmony. The effect is of some stately and solemn proceeding: slow, sparse, deep. At length, a new keyboard sound emerges, in time developing into a stretched-out solo; these notes drift like the piece itself. It is not clear yet what environment the listener might be in, but there is not the isolation of deep space as evoked on *Zeit*: this is more like a bare, remote, terrestrial location.

As an organ takes up the solo part, the music shifts gear until new high cutoff sounds emerge, so that two keyboard lines start to intertwine. Now, both volume and emotional intensity are increased a notch. The first solo acquires speed and resolution until a new, more metallic keyboard opens up: most likely Baumann's Rhodes. The listener, however, remains in the same desolate environment. The Rhodes' deep tremolo indicates tension and suspense; a hint of danger.

Though still drifting, a new synthesizer sound indicates deepening tension through its volume and choice of notes: semitones indicating tension. But this does not last long. It is as if a visitor has appeared in the environment, immediately to depart. But after this section, a new sound emerges – VCS3 chatter like alien birdsong – which somehow moves the listener on. Perhaps this is new company. Echo and reverb give the sounds depth as the keyboards drift and sway. In time, the keyboards begin a new theme of more urgency, rolling chords and upper-register notes, all shimmering; a firm sign of movement.

White noise whooshes signal the arrival of new forms, indicated by a change in the VCS3 pattern as the chords underneath boom and roll. The listener is now in a new environment, similar to the opening one, but with much more activity. The mood is akin to that of 'Fauni-Gena', evoking an alien landscape via meandering keyboard chords; the mood weird, sparse, half-eerie – the noise of electric creatures.

With the return of the Rhodes and another drifting keyboard solo (its timbre not unlike that of Rick Wright's early sound), a new section develops, this time mirrored by a vocal-based keyboard. The listener now seems to be in a firmer, harder environment, albeit one containing little except weird life forms – an alien planet then, or something like it. The Rhodes is particularly effective here, making full use of its metallic timbres and tremolo.

Suddenly, a sequence opens up, and in a few moments, it has taken over the piece. All the accompanying keyboards follow it, including Mellotron strings. Delay brought in later adds depth to this rhythmic element. Soon, a full-scale sequenced piece is under way, with all the classic Tangerine Dream elements. The Mellotron strings are effective here, with a high-register synth in counterpoint. As a very early indication of what Franke could and would go on to do with the Moog sequencer, this is a fantastic bit of improvisation which works perfectly. At its conclusion, the sequences tighten up a little and the Mellotron flutes take over, until, at the end, a great chord washes over the music, leaving just echoed, oscillating sequences and a thunking sound put through a heavy spring reverb.

Part two of the concert opens with pulsing white noise, overlaid with spectral keyboard washes, which themselves begin to spiral and turn as their timbres change. Then the white noise mutates into an eight-note sequence, set firm around its root note, this element alone for a while before new elements arrive. Soon, the music is in full flow, with tension, excitement and strangeness: the classic live sound of the mid-1970s, with the Moog ascendant.

As the sequences die back a little, a new keyboard sound emerges, phased and ominous, above which VCS3 oscillations flutter. This section is a little like *Rubycon.* Slowly, the music develops, the keyboards trading themes and elongated solos, the VCS3 twittering away, the Mellotron changing to flutes and strings. As the sequence alters to 5/4 time, new timbres and accompanying keyboards emerge, usually to die away, leaving space for new sounds. A change to 6/4 and a woozy new frequency shift then brings a kind of sonic drunkenness to the music.

By the time Franke has changed the time signature to 2/4 and then 3/4, the music is bouncing in any and all directions. Soon though, the sequences fade back – diminishing, albeit still transmuting, leaving a solitary organ, whose timbres shift and mutate below an echo effect. Mellotron strings soon accompany this organ, bringing a majestic vibe to the conclusion of the sequenced improvisation, which, at its very end, changes into a series of upward flights of pitch and timbre. The remainder of the piece drifts into keyboard washes and echoed VCS3 oscillations.

The thirteen-minute encore is based around deeply echoed sounds and keyboard textures, all of them bouncing and loping, as if trapped inside their respective synthesizers. When these noises cease, the music feeds into a drone, against which various eerie sounds are pitted. One of these sounds mutates into a fast sequence as an organ swells beneath it. As the music continues, the vibe remains light, almost playful, with the keyboards echoing the classic Rick Wright sound in places. There is no density here, no tension. Over the remainder of the piece there are changes in direction and feel, but little more development, concluding with drifting keyboard textures, chattering VCS3s and audience applause.

This superb recording (direct off the original master tape, recorded with Virgin's Manor Mobile) is a delight to hear in such high quality: another welcome bonus on the *In Search Of Hades* set.

Live At The Rainbow, London

Personnel:
Edgar Froese: Mellotron, VCS3 synthesizer
Chris Franke: Moog synthesizer, keyboards, VCS3 synthesizer
Peter Baumann: organ, electric piano, VCS3 synthesizer
Recorded by the Manor Mobile: 26th October 1974
Mixer: Ben Wiseman (2018)
Release dates: UK and US: October 2019
Chart placings: -
Running time: 119:21 (Two discs)
All tracks by Froese, Franke, Baumann
Tracks: 1. 'Part 1' 2. 'Part 2' 3. 'Part 3' 4. 'Encore'

This concert begins with John Peel's introduction, his first words remarking on the lack of the Bay City Rollers as support. Peel then goes into a typically meandering story, of playing *Phaedra* whilst driving – so great to hear his voice again! – then more about how wonderful it was that Tangerine Dream confounded expectations with the LP's critical and commercial success.

The music opens with droning, low-register keyboards before heading off into organ-fuelled territory. The listener might be in space, or perhaps just floating up high. As harmonies and extrapolations begin, the tone of the music becomes a little more dense, conveyed by Baumann's Rhodes electric piano, which – as at the Victoria Palace gig – is brilliantly utilised. When a ghostly Mellotron choir part enters the mix and the Rhodes goes a little off-key, the listener is again transported to one of those marvellously woozy, uncertain, eerie landscapes which the group were so adept at evoking.

Mellotron flutes and a cycling VCS3 sound convey the listener to a new part of the sky, before more weird off-key sounds enter, followed by Mellotron strings accompanying a Moog sequence. This sequence dips and dives through the mix, never constant. It is uncertain musical territory full of sonic unknowns, though one that offers the listener a sense of great expectation. In due course, the sequence and its supporting chords stabilise around a root note, and the improvisation is off and away. The group were often brilliant at making these moves from drift to flow, coalescing in marvellous, almost telepathic unison around the appropriate key.

Bass thrums and heavy Mellotron strings anchor the subsequent music (a premonition of 1977 and *Encore* here) until the key rises and the keyboards acquire phased effects. Now the sequence becomes a bubbling rhythm which fades and reappears again, sometimes to phased keyboards, sometimes to VCS3 oscillations.

At the twenty-minute mark, everything dies away, leaving only high-register keyboards. It is suddenly tranquil; the music has departed the auditorium. What remains is weird, imprecise and unknowable. This odd *Alice-In-Wonderland* section continues until the Mellotron flutes pick up the main part. Yet now the ticking synth sounds like a surreal electronic clock...

In due course, the muscles of the music return, conveyed in the most part by Mellotron strings, to which other keyboards add runs and chords. A great, dense swathe of sound builds, rooted in one key, but occasionally rising or falling, though this eventually transmutes into white noise and echoed VCS3 sounds, ending with bubbling sequences and more filtered white noise. The vibe remains surreal, albeit rather heavy – more Dali than Dodgson – ending with a hint of the surreal clock and much applause.

'Part 2' begins with deep reverb on the VCS3 noise before a metallic sound – repeated like the thwack of a steel whip – opens up. The listener is inside some kind of sonic chamber; strange, perhaps dangerous. When an organ theme sounds, it is like a rescue, conveyed also by new sequences on Franke's Moog. The chamber has dissolved and the listener is flying once again, although not for long.

As keyboard timbres come to dominate the music, the vibe enters a new dynamic phase. Sequences swirl, noises echo, synths oscillate. Then a precise two-note sequence begins, around which sounds thrum and bubble: sonic boom, sonic fluids. At length, the improvisation settles around a key, which the Mellotron choir and strings in particular develop.

The piece ends with high-register organ sounds layered around the final sequenced section, which, at its conclusion, ends deep and bassy, paired with a mournful Mellotron flute.

'Part 3' is another full-scale improvisation, clocking in at 38 minutes. Opening with a drifting organ drone – as of a futuristic funeral parlour – the music slowly heads off into more cosmic territory, again evoking flight or floating, the listener passing through an audio welkin.

After a while, Baumann's Rhodes begins to pick up a new mood, supported by VCS3 twitter and the funereal organ chords. The piece remains soft and stately, however, enlivened only by occasional flourishes on the organ. As a rhythmic element enters the mix, the vibe picks up – a sonic procession perhaps, though not at speed. New keyboards begin to take up new themes, with one three-note riff dominating, though this mutates into a solo peppered with a tinkling synth accompaniment, which itself mutates into a deeper register, taking on its own rhythm. This is another fabulous change from ambience to flow, beautifully played – mixer Ben Wiseman skilfully bringing it out from the original multitrack tape.

Now the music is in bouncing full flow, the keyboards light and airy, the music evoking a Terry Riley minimal feel, especially through the rhythmic organ. It is like the group's homage to Riley's 'A Rainbow In Curved Air', though this sensation passes as more dreamlike elements emerge. This is a particularly gorgeous section, showing the trio's improvisational and musical skills in full.

In due course, new sounds appear, notably a plucked solo sound supported by bass notes and a new organ section. The bouncing, minimal feel, however, is retained, echoing Terry Riley again, or perhaps even Steve Reich, who by the end of 1974 was being noticed by a wider audience (nearly a decade later, Froese would bring a more obvious Reich influence to the group's music). When this section ends, the music flows into keyboard drifts which swirl, descend and rise.

As the Mellotron strings bring a more earthly tone, the music – augmented by bass notes – enters a relaxed, drifting coda, to which VCS3 oscillations are added. Soon, the mood is returned to one of floating, evoked by VCS3 and the Mellotron alone. Some parts of this section echo Froese's *Phaedra* Mellotron piece 'Mysterious Semblance At The Strand Of Nightmares'.

The music concludes with a brief sequenced section, above which Froese continues his Mellotron meanderings. At the end, all that remains is white noise, filtered sequences and Mellotron flutes – enigmatic, cycling, cosmic – a beautiful ending, which diminishes to audience applause.

The encore begins with more cosmic twittering, underpinned by a subtle drone that resolves into a one-note sequence. Now it is the Mellotron choir's turn to add texture. As the sequence acquires a higher register, VCS3 fluttering overlays the sound before the sequence returns to its heavy, doom-laden origin, albeit now of two notes. Still, the Mellotron choir lays chords above it all.

Halfway through, the improvisation is in full flow. Froese varies the Mellotron choir, pulling it apart into three chords which stab and decay. In due course, a new solo rises, but it is lighter, played with more buoyancy, and the sequences accommodate this by adding echo. When the Mellotron strings come in, the mood is much lighter, as if heavy, dark curtains have been drawn to reveal sunlight.

As the piece concludes, the key changes – rising, ascending – while all the accompanying elements also become drunk, chaotic as if evoking sudden ascent through the sky. After this, the key settles again, but the music has a note of peril, evoked in particular via the sequence. A high-tremolo synth above this adds to the sense of danger. Soon though, the Mellotron reverts to a major key, bringing stability for the listener... and a hint of *Sorcerer* to come. With the sequences gathering pace and rising in pitch and key, more chaos enters the music until it dissolves into Mellotron stabs and nothingness... then more applause.

The sound quality of this notable concert is fantastic, with full use made of Mark Powell's access to the original Manor Mobile tapes. It is a significant addition to the collection of live recordings from this iconic period.

Elsewhere, the group played Sheffield City Hall three days after the Rainbow (released on the orange *Bootleg Box Set Volume 1*); North East

London Polytechnic on 6 November; Plymouth Guildhall on 9 November; the Kelvin Hall in Glasgow on 20 November, and St George's Hall in Bradford on 26 November. All in all, there were twenty dates on this momentous tour.

In his 2020 musicradar.com interview, Baumann recalled how the group approached live work, explaining that they had no wish to recreate their studio albums:

> A live show for us was a chance to play some more music. As the concerts got bigger and we started doing proper tours, there were occasional themes ... that reappeared, but nothing more than that. If we started playing and the music suddenly went off in this direction, we would follow it.

As the group soon found out, many of their instruments were not suited to the live environment. In the same interview, Baumann recalled their fragility and unreliability:

> That became part of the live show. It was live ... things went wrong ... quite a lot. Sometimes, they went really wrong. Sometimes, they went really right. Sometimes, the first part of the show would be fantastic, the middle bit was okay and the ending was lousy. We honestly never knew how it was going to turn out. But we were okay with that. It was exciting. There wasn't much we could do about it, so we went on playing, hoping that an extra-cool part would overshadow the not-so-good part.

In the same interview, Baumann recalled the group's instruments:

> The M400 Mellotron, the Fender Rhodes, the Moog 3P, the Synthi, the Elka Rhapsody, the ARP 2600. But, very early on, we started to go down our own path. We hired a company in Berlin and developed our own unique sequencers. Four units, all fitted into a big rig.

Towards the end of summer, however, a new kind of project arrived. *Oedipus Tyrannus* was a play adapted by Keith Mitchell to be staged at the Chichester Festival on 18 August. In June, Tangerine Dream went into CBS Studios in London to record the soundtrack to this play, but the music was later archived to go down in lore as a *lost* recording. In fact, parts of the recording were used in later albums, including *Rubycon* and *Encore.*

But some outsiders *did* hear the music, including John Peel, who played a couple of excerpts on his 11 July radio show. The soundtrack exists in the form of an overture and three acts, with most of the recordings given their first release on the *In Search Of Hades* CD box set.

Oedipus Tyrannus (2019)

Personnel:
Edgar Froese: Mellotron, VCS3 synthesizer
Chris Franke: Moog synthesizer, keyboards, VCS3 synthesizer
Peter Baumann: organ, electric piano, VCS3 synthesizer, flute
Producer: Tangerine Dream and Steve Taylor
Recorded at CBS Studio 2, London: June 1974
Release date: UK: October 2019
Chart placing: -
Running time: 74:45
All tracks by Froese, Franke, Baumann
Tracks: 1. 'Overture' 2. 'Act 1' 3. 'Act 2: Battle' 4. 'Act 2: Baroque' 5. 'Act 2: Zeus' 6. 'Act 3'

The eleven-minute overture opens with dense, mysterious chords recorded normally, then, along with other keyboard sounds, turned backwards by reversing the tape direction. This opening section fades into eerie atmospherics reminiscent of parts of *Rubycon,* before a more obvious tape speed effect enters the mix with a number of gloriously eerie synthesized calls. Spectral chords appear in the reverberated rear of the piece, but they rarely last for more than a few seconds. Still the backwards sounds continue – piano mostly, sometimes played by hitting the strings, as with a santur. At length, a Mellotron enters, signalling a section of music well known to fans of *Encore.* As the overture concludes, the Mellotron takes up a part above which a plaintive synth solo appears, bringing the piece to its denouement. This overture is a marvellous piece of atmospheric music, showing the sophisticated compositional and technical level the group were now working on.

'Act 1' opens with mysterious knocking and scraping sounds, before an ominous drone and its accompanying gliss guitar begin to sound; tinkling keyboards laid over the top. There are definite hints of the sound world of *Zeit* in this opening: cold, remote. After a while, the gliss guitar rises higher in the mix, VCS3 oscillations occasionally counterpointing. Slowly, the density and intensity of the music rises, until it reaches an enigmatic plateau, where – bathed in gliss and VCS3 – it rests for a while. With the return of the tinkling keyboard, the music drifts away, keyboards taking the place of the gliss guitar for a more sumptuous sound. Again, this is a wonderfully atmospheric piece.

The first section of 'Act 2' opens with filtered white noise sounding like a steam train, before a high feedback echo takes other sounds into cyclical repetition. As the white noise turns into a distinct rhythm, other harsher sounds enter, until the music moves forward with some energy. Then a three-note sequence joins the rhythm, treated with a delay to give it movement, as with the mid-1970s albums and concerts. Soon, deeply-phased Mellotron chords join in, turning it into a classic Tangerine Dream piece, which then lopes off on its sonic journey to the accompaniment of other keyboards, all of them either filtered or phased. Against this complex mélange, VCS3 oscillations bounce, topping the music off to perfection, evoking the sense of battle given in the title.

The second section opens with sparse, drifting, low-register keyboard chords, before a melancholy Mellotron flute and a simple plucked synth sound arrive, the latter playing a baroque theme, the Mellotron accompanying it. Against this section, what sounds like Baumann's *Phaedra* recorder or flute (he is listed as having played flute on the recordings) can be heard, evoking some enigmatic period of baroque history. With reverb and a little echo, this is a moving, almost elegiac part. In due course, the rhythm fades and the Mellotron drifts off almost on its own – just simple, quiet chords accompanying it. These chords, however, develop into something more plangent, each one circulating around the other so that the music seems to cycle in abstract space.

The third section of 'Act 2' opens with keyboards and synths familiar to lovers of *Encore* – mysterious reverberated and echoed sounds, beautifully arranged to maximum eerie effect. This sonic collage plays for six minutes, evoking the enigma of Zeus and his stratagems.

'Act 3' is over twenty minutes of music, beginning with dense chords and Mellotron flute, which would later be reused for the finale of *Rubycon*. In the book accompanying the *In Search Of Hades* box set, researched and written by Wouter Bessels, a photograph of a scrawled note on the tape reel box confirms this. It is surely one of the group's most beautiful compositions: sheer perfection, not least the extraordinary shimmering note which emerges almost three minutes in and then drops, resetting the whole key of the piece. Soon however the music drifts off into a new section, led by the Mellotron flute and deeper keyboards, all of them rotating around one another to glorious effect. At length, white noise enters the mix, and the listener seems to be transported back down to earth, having floated in the skies. New VCS3 sounds begin, all of them deep, dense and dark, adding mystery to the mood. With the departure of the keyboards, all that is left is abstract sound and noise, given depth by reverb. Soon, however, the hint of a drone and a new set of drifting keyboards overlay the noise, suggesting a new mood. The atmosphere is now eerie, hinting even at madness through the macabre nature of the VCS3 sounds, which in due course are accompanied by scratching and clonking sounds. Meanwhile, the drone develops into a series of unrelated notes, again indicating delusional, even chaotic motions or mental activity. Mellotron chords added soon after increase the feel of insanity – there is no fixed key to this piece; all is fragmented, albeit held together by the strength of the musical vision. Further VCS3 noise arrives, but then the music clears a little, the hint of a stable key arriving, along with a chiming, oscillating synth... but then the madness returns and the music turns again, this time underpinned by another series of keyboard chords. After a few minutes, all that is left is white noise and VCS3 chatter, before a spiky Moog sequence emerges, one that bridges *Phaedra* and *Rubycon* in its sounds and choice of rhythm. Mellotron strings and other keyboards are added to this sequence, until the piece becomes another classic group work familiar to all fans of this period. At the music's conclusion, deeper reverb is applied to the Moog sequence and oscillating VCS3 noise bathes the piece, turning structure to the formless electronic void. At length, what remains is chaos and a mass of blips and bleeps suffused with white noise and reverb, which, in departing, fade into reverb alone.

Oedipus Tyrannus is perhaps the most important *lost* Tangerine Dream recording, one justly lauded when it was finally given a release in 2019. As a document of those times it is fascinating, but as music it is in places breathtaking, showing the strides the group had taken along their chosen trajectory.

So far, the group had acquired a good reputation, with only a few bad reviews in the music press, written by sneering pop and blues devotees. In December however, at the only French concert of the year, Tangerine Dream would encounter a new phenomenon: notoriety.

The Rheims Cathedral concert of 13 December was part of a tour of cathedrals the band undertook as their reputation increased. It was the first rock concert ever given at a European religious institution. With a highly successful year almost finished, the omens looked good for another foray into new environments and new music.

The reality was somewhat different. Close to 6,000 fans were permitted to attend the concert: more than Rheims Cathedral was able to hold. As a result of this, some fans left the cathedral in less-than-perfect condition, with the most notorious incidents (although exaggerated after the event) being attendees urinating against stone pillars. Following the concert, the Catholic church forbade further rock concerts at its properties.

The press took hold of the incident with fervour. Reports were everywhere – in national papers and in local ones. The *Newcastle Evening Chronicle* of 17 December was a typical example:

> ANGRY parishioners of Rheims Cathedral today called for its purification, claiming it was desecrated during a pop music concert in the building last Friday. Those who condemned the staging of the pop concert given by the Tangerine Dream group, said that 5,000 youths had desecrated the 12th-century cathedral. They claimed pop fans left litter everywhere, smoked hashish and urinated in the cathedral used for the coronation of French kings. A group of worshippers said in a statement issued in Rheims: 'The church is a place of worship and not a festival hall ... it is abnormal that the archbishop should allow pagan music to be played there. The cathedral was transformed into a smoking den, and drug-and-alcohol orgies took place.

Needless to say, those orgies never happened. Even in America the incident acquired notoriety, though one report in the *Marshfield News-Herald* six days afterwards offered a more realistic assessment of what happened:

> Wasn't That Bad. REIMS, France (AP): 'Pot-smoking teenagers may have desecrated Reims Cathedral, but Easter-weekend worshippers leave the church in worse condition', Abbot Charles Phililonat said today. The abbot, who is the cathedral's archpriest, responded to demands by parishioners for purification of the 13th-century cathedral where French kings were crowned. The parishioners said members of a Friday rock concert audience of 5,000, drank, smoked marijuana and urinated in the cathedral. The archpriest deplored the use of the drug, but added, 'I participated in cleaning up after the concert, and there were no syringes

> as some people maintained. There were only three or four wine bottles and the rest were for sodas and fruit juice. The Reims Cathedral is much dirtier after Easter weekend, for example'.

Yet even *Phaedra,* plus a British tour, plus Reims, was not enough for Edgar Froese. He had plans for a solo album.

Recordings had commenced in Berlin in November of the previous year, ending in March 1974. Released in June – just four months after *Phaedra* – the album *Aqua* was another groundbreaking electronic work, also split into four pieces, with two on each side. The music resembled that of Froese's group, but there were differences, including an important technical difference. Using the binaural technique, side B was designed to be an especially good listen on stereo headphones: the so-called 'artificial head' system of Gunther Brunschen. The music itself was impressionistic and occasionally dramatic – as with the second piece 'Panorphelia' – with 'NGC 891' benefitting from Franke's Moog. As with much of the group's artwork, Froese's wife Monique provided the cover image.

The album is highly respected by fans of electronic music and easily stands in the same league as most of the group's music.

1974 was a pivotal year for Tangerine Dream. Creative success, artistic fulfillment, commercial success, a lengthy tour, money for a Moog, radio-play, artistic commissions and even a little notoriety all combined to bring Froese, Franke and Baumann much satisfaction. The schedule had been hectic, but it had been worth it. The following year would see the group ascend to even greater heights, including an album recognised by many as perhaps their all-time greatest.

1975 – Gigs, Australia, Gigs

There is nothing like success for breeding success. 1975 dawned exceedingly bright for Tangerine Dream. In January, they recorded what would become one of their most lauded, most loved and most influential albums.

The instrumentation was much the same as on *Phaedra,* with the addition of extras like piano and gong. Recordings progressed well, and there were fewer technical difficulties. One of the most notable changes, however – evident on the stunning side A – was Franke's use of the Moog sequencer. Franke was not the first person to use the Moog in the way he did, but he was the first to use its adaptive rhythmic and melodic possibilities in live situations. In addition, his insight and proficiency as a musician allowed him to realise the Moog's possibilities.

The adaptive method of playing involves setting the sequencer running at a particular tempo with the chosen voltage-controlled oscillators operating, then triggering notes using a keyboard. With enough skill and judgement, and with delay units thickening and multiplying the sequence notes, the basis of what became known as Berlin School music is set. Nobody had done anything like it until Franke. By playing different notes in differently-numbered clusters (two notes for a two-note sequence, three for a three-note sequence, a four-note chord for a four-note sequence, and so on) with the delay set to match the tempo (e.g., half-time, or more dramatically, 3/2 time), a vast array of sequenced music could be made – at once stable and structured, yet open to variation of all kinds simply by choosing different chords, triads etc.

Many musicians made use of this technique following Franke's pioneering work, including Ashra, with whom Klaus Schulze had worked. But perhaps the most exceptional example of the style was to appear three years later with an album made by Michael Hoenig – with whom Franke had been part of Agitation Free – who deputised for Baumann on the upcoming Australian tour. *Departure From The Northern Wasteland* is certainly the equal of *Rubycon,* and for many fans of the genre it is the pinnacle Berlin School work. The album, Hoenig's only serious venture into the field, is loved by thousands.

In an interview given to Mark Prendergast for the 1994 *Tangents* collection, Froese recalled recording *Rubycon* at the Manor in Oxfordshire:

> When the band walked into the Manor for the second time, we were weighted down by the pressure of the success of *Phaedra*. There was a pressure to do it again, but one has to point out that Simon Draper (the producer) and Richard Branson at Virgin did not pressure us to be commercial ... Tangerine Dream could do whatever they wanted to on record, which was a very unusual practice for a record company.

In an interview given to issue 6 of *Tangenten* in 1994, Froese elaborated:

> When we did *Rubycon*, we talked much about if we wanted a commercial success or if we wanted to be progressive on our own terms. And honestly, we decided that it was mostly ourselves it was all about. We wanted to develop the music we liked the most, and to express ourselves personally.

In the same interview, Froese explained how the success and technical knowledge of the previous year set them up:

> The recording of *Rubycon* was a very floating process. Unlike the *Phaedra* production, there was never a break in the creative flow. The band had been on tour for most of the previous year and was now hot to spend a month working on some new music. Because of the commercial success of *Phaedra*, the sequencers could now be technically better-equipped. At that time, this branch of technology was fairly unknown, and any technical alterations had to be custom-built ... most of our earnings went into new equipment.

Rubycon was both easier to record and stimulated by an improved technical setting, though one that was still bedevilled by glitches and problems. Yet the album betrayed none of these issues. It was a sublime journey across a brand new musical landscape, albeit one haunted by the spectre of something from Froese's childhood: war.

Rubycon (1975)

Personnel:

Edgar Froese: Mellotron, guitar, VCS3 synthesizer, organ, gong

Chris Franke: double Moog synthesizer, Synthi A, organ, Elka organ, prepared piano, gong

Peter Baumann: organ, EMS Synthi A, Fender Rhodes, prepared piano, voice,

ARP 2600
Producer: Tangerine Dream
Recorded at the Manor, Oxfordshire: January 1975
Release dates: UK and US: March 1975
Chart placings: UK: 10
Running time: 34:53
Side One: 1. 'Rubycon, Part I' (Tangerine Dream)
Side Two: 1. 'Rubycon, Part II' (Tangerine Dream)

The album is split into two side-long pieces, 'Part I' opening with ominous, fluttering chords from a keyboard that sounds as though it has emerged from an underground lair, over which are laid soft enigmatic notes. Under a wandering phased melody, shifting chords alter the key in mysterious fashion. Other deeply reverberated sounds rise and fall, and a majestic choir chord and phased string sounds begin, before the first main theme of the piece emerges, bringing with it light: a kind of sonic dawn after interminable night. Additional synth fragments sound like the vocalisations of underwater creatures, underpinned by Mellotron strings and the wandering melody, occasionally augmented by a Mellotron choir.

As the sonic wash diminishes to a thin, echoed sound, all that is left is a bass drone sounding like some aeroplane of war emerging from dawn's parting clouds. It is a spine-tingling return to the sense of foreboding after the glory of dawn, echoing the Froese family's World War II experience – also evoking the sense of shattered, chaotic catastrophe that was Germany after the end of the conflict. Further echoed synths accompany this drone, before the first sequence begins: a four-note descending ostinato in the deeper registers of Franke's Moog. This sequence develops, with Franke changing the pattern from four per bar to six per bar, in the adaptive method used in this period. Against it, the second main theme emerges, played again on a Mellotron, with plenty of phasing effect. Against this ominous backdrop, Baumann's Fender Rhodes notes arrive, dropping in then vanishing, returning in higher registers, before – without warning – the sequence changes rhythm and the underlying chord descends a tone, introducing a brief and tremendously dramatic interlude, before the next sequenced section begins.

Against this new sequence, the listener hears what seems like clattering bone percussion, adding drama to an already dramatic piece. Now the sequence returns to a variant of the first four-note pattern. New, strangely metallic synth sounds parallel the sequence, as piano, Mellotron and synths all rise and fall in an evocation of some majestic, extraordinary vision. White noise percussion adds to the ever-thickening mix, before once again the descended-chord interlude returns, this time twice, leading to a slight reduction in intensity.

After the weight and dark drama of the central section, the sequence pattern calms, and a piano enters the mix as the sequence shifts up an octave. This is a lighter section; a lifting of the tension of the main piece. Here, following that change in mood, the sequence changes to a 3/4 time signature, then 2/4 as the music breaks down, dispersing into what is left of the day. Synth chords emerge, washing away the main piece's dread, ushering in a lighter, more hopeful conclusion.

Here, Franke and Baumann used prepared piano sounds modified with a tremolo effect to take over the music and lead it into a harrowing coda. This sound – discovered by The Beatles, and famously used by Richard Wright for the opening of Pink Floyd's 'Echoes' – was created by amplifying a grand piano and putting the sound through a Leslie speaker and a delay unit. Franke and Baumann extracted metallic, almost painful sounds using this technique, giving again to this first part of the album the feeling that something dreadful is nearby.

This side is a masterclass in musical tension, much of it evoking the sense of something ominous about to occur, yet which never actually happens, contrasted with sections of more a optimistic mood, notably at the beginning. Using comparatively simple sequences and a range of organs, keyboards, piano, and Froese's VCS3 synth, the trio build up one of their greatest musical moments.

'Part II' opens with a hair-raising siren created on synths, again echoing the dreadful memory of war in Germany. Somehow this sound takes the listener away from the first part's nameless dread, albeit replacing it with something equally menacing: the threat of imminent destruction. Dense bass chords and sound effects underpin the siren, like the winds of war: the terror and the horror. Occasional Mellotron choir inserts seem like the cries of innumerable victims. It is an extraordinarily effective opening, not least because of the siren's wavering pitch giving the sound a surreal, hallucinatory quality at once akin to, yet far removed from, a real siren.

As this part finishes, the timbre changes to something a little lighter, as a new key emerges, and with it a new sequence. Faster than the sequence of 'Part 1', and with more attack, this sequence bounces between time signatures as Franke's adaptive technique makes quicksilver alterations in rhythm and time – far more variation than on side A. Mellotron strings come in, adding colour and a brand-new melodic theme above which light synth effects come and go.

After a few minutes, Froese's guitar enters, recorded backwards with additional post-recording effects so that the end result is more like a synth than a guitar. Above and around this dense musicality, Franke's sequences ripple and mutate, never staying the same. Partway through, there is even a key change, though that swiftly returns to its original form, as again Froese's backwards guitar and additional synths vie for the listener's attention – all the time calling out via the third theme: a shout for freedom amidst war and destruction.

In due course, the key changes again, and new sonic elements emerge: aquatic synth effects, deeply reverberated Mellotron chords and more backwards guitar. This section – so much faster than the music on the first side – evokes the chaotic flight of the victims of war: running headlong, hurrying this way and that almost at random, a sensation evoked by Franke's pattering sequenced ostinatos.

But soon, this section is over. The sequences vanish and great washes of phased keyboard dominate the mix: perhaps sanctuary at the end of flight. Phased and delayed sea recordings (recorded on the south coast of England and played back on two tape machines of varying speed) arrive, and then the listener is in an entirely new and different environment, where peace has broken out. Not long afterwards comes proof of that peace – a thrumming chord, wistful synth effects, and the unmistakable sound of the Mellotron flute, which here is used to evoke rest; perhaps even closure. Beneath this Mellotron the synths ebb and flow, dying away to reveal the thrumming chord again – mutating, transforming and returning. Then comes one of the great Tangerine Dream moments, a spine-tingling chord change, bass deep as if out of profound depths, giving the listener a sense of the end of the journey; rest and tranquillity, with no sign of war, conflict, pursuit or danger. This section, as revealed by Wouter Bessels in the book accompanying the 2019 release *In Search Of Hades,* was taken from the recordings for *Oedipus Tyrannus*.

All that is left after this is the Mellotron flute and wispy keyboard chords, reverberating into increasing distance, taking the listener further away from everything that has occurred – a sonic message of peace, even of hope. At length, the music fades to nothing on a final flute note.

This album set the tone for all Berlin School musicians who were to follow, yet none have captured the depth of mood and emotion these three musicians brought to *Rubycon*. That they were German had everything to do with the feelings and emotions they wished to evoke. A few followers have come close to *Rubycon,* but apart from Michael Hoenig, none have equalled it, nor will they ever. This album was a first, and like many first explorations of new ground its genius is in that novelty. There can only be one *Rubycon*.

The album's cover was not quite as abstract as earlier designs, though it had one feature in common with them – a tiny image of Froese's son Jerome, which had been used in various sizes and incarnations since *Alpha Centauri*. In Johnny Black's *ThisBEAT* interview of April 1986, Froese's wife Monique said the following of the cover: 'I think *Rubycon* is my favourite cover design because it is so simple; just one single droplet of water splashing onto the surface. I also like *Tangram,* because that's even simpler'. Froese elaborated in the same interview:

> Monique likes simplicity in all things. We've rarely put our own image on our record sleeves; not because we think we're so ugly, but our faces cannot explain what the music is about, so why put them on? Just because people like to identify with the personalities? They should really identify with the music.

The critical reception for *Rubycon* was positive, recognising its scope, depth and originality, and supporting its iconic status. But 1975 was not just a year of creative success in the studio. In Australia, *Phaedra* had been certified as a gold album, which resulted in a tour being put together. Nine dates in Australia and one in New Zealand were played, with Michael Hoenig deputising for Baumann. Venues included the Dallas Brooks Hall in Melbourne on 13 March and Adelaide's Festival Theatre on 25 March.

As March turned into April, however, the group played a concert destined to be beloved of thousands of their fans: London's Royal Albert Hall on 2 April. For this gig, Hoenig was still the third keyboards man. John Peel introduced the event, and the whole thing was recorded by the BBC. In later years, the much-missed rock DJ Tommy Vance would play excerpts from it on his *Friday Rock Show*, but apart from taped bootlegs the first proper release was on the orange *Bootleg Box Set Volume 1* collection. The superior Manor Mobile recording appeared on the *In Search Of Hades* set.

Over the years, Michael Hoenig's presence in the group, and at this concert in particular, has generated a lot of interest in how it came about and what happened. In issue 2 of his *Neumusik* fanzine, David Elliott interviewed Hoenig, who gave an insight into the period. He was first asked about his reaction to joining the group. Was he pleased?: 'Well, no. Because it's always a terrible situation for a musician to come into a band where there exists fixed standards that developed over a long period of time: standards you have to adjust to'.

He was asked about the Australian tour and what the reaction was like:

> A very good reaction. That tour was pretty good. We played together really well. Christoph, for me, is fantastic: maybe the best partner I could ever play with, because he's fast and precise. I have an immediate language with him, in both musical and technical terms. Each concert had around 5,000 people, which was pretty good. But for me, I was a little depressed with certain aspects. For me, it was the first tour where the contact with the audience was completely broken. It was just the typical pop star business: hotel, limousine, backstage, curtain opens, and you play your set, jump back into the limousine and get back to the hotel. Well, maybe that's normal, but I felt terrible.

Hoenig also spoke about not recording with the group:

> The problem was, I was supposed to go into the studio with them for *Rubycon*. My publisher in those days didn't let me. That was solely a juristic problem ... As soon as we had played the Albert Hall in London, I quitted them. As I said, I wanted to make pieces on my own. I just felt that after five years of being with groups, we were having those typical human problems – I knew that number completely, from my days with Agitation Free, and I didn't want that all over again.

Froese recalled preparations for the concert, and for others he had played, in an interview broadcast on Radio 2 on 17 December 1997:

> We put our headsets on one ear, and then we were listening to the tone of the Mellotron while (we had) already started playing our stuff. Then, by listening to the 440 Hz out of the oscillator, we were tuning the Mellotron against it ... and that had to be done about ten times during the gig of two and a half hours. Looking back to those days, that sort of adventurous fear, not knowing if you will overcome a good, a bad concert, out-of-tune concert, or whatever. Today, everything, it's much

better-tuned, it's nearly perfect, but it's not having a wild ride through the jungle anymore.

In the same interview, Froese recalled the extraordinary events preceding the Royal Albert Hall gig:

A couple of hours prior to the start of the gig, someone came along and said, 'They (the Musicians' Union) are asking for a couple of thousand pounds for you're using an orchestra. You are not using *them*, you are using your bloody keys here. *That's* an orchestra'. So there was a bit of a fight going on backstage, and so we had to pay something that night.

In his interview with Mark Prendergast for the 1994 *Tangents* box set, Froese explained the issues with keyboards and with his beloved Mellotron in particular:

I had orchestral instruments recorded by the BBC for my Mellotron, at the time a very luxurious thing to do. One can hear an oboe on 'Rubycon, Part II', as well as numerous strings sections and horns. The biggest problem, however, was the inconstant power supply at the Manor. At the time, there were electrical problems throughout the Oxford region, and sometimes the power was cut off for two to three hours at a time. We had to interrupt recording sessions when this happened, to connect our synths to electrical generators. Chris' Moog often played completely random sequences because of the unstable electrical current driving the oscillators ... When we finished recording, there were altogether twelve hours of music from which to mix the final master.

Musician Peter Beasley – active for a long time on the British electronic music scene – attended the Royal Albert Hall concert:

I recorded the gig on a cheap cassette recorder, but the tape was stolen some years later. Luckily, I also recorded the BBC Radio London mono broadcast and band interviews from April 1975. Still, 28 years was a long time to wait for the official release on the *Bootleg Box Set Volume 1*. The undoubted highlight of this set is the capture of the complete Royal Albert Hall concert, excellently recorded by the BBC. It is part two (39 minutes) of the concert which stands out. For me, it is the greatest piece of improvisation TD ever did. After a long slow, dark Mellotron

> buildup, the sequencer emerges like a bulldozer clearing its way across a landscape. The piece reaches a stunning climax, with sequencers, lead lines and powerful percussives, before giving way to a tranquil Mellotron-choir-and-flute ending. Much of the credit to the success of the Royal Albert Hall recording must go to Michael Hoenig (shamefully uncredited), who was in the band far too briefly whilst Peter Baumann went walkabout. I was lucky enough to be at the Royal Albert Hall that night and had a birds-eye view of Hoenig, and I could see how much he contributed to the overall sound. Certainly, Hoenig made a significant contribution to the gig, and I still rate the second half the finest improvisation they ever did.

Musician Stephen Bradbury of Black Tempest also recalled attending this iconic concert:

> I remember incense burning along the front of the stage, Peelie doing his MC thing, and cheese plants (Monstera) dotted around the stage. After the intro, the stage was darkened, except for UV lights. Then the lights on one sequencer started rolling across, then another sequencer, then another – it was magical.

British fans were a crucial part of this phase of the group's success. Two years of extensive touring across the country spawned many remarkable gigs. Dave Bessell of the much-lauded band Node remembered the Liverpool Cathedral gig on 16 October:

> The Anglican Cathedral in Liverpool was crammed with a rather unusual congregation to hear Tangerine Dream. To their credit, the church's representative – who welcomed everyone before the music started – was unreservedly sympathetic to the crowd, and seemed oblivious to the thick clouds of 'exotic smoke' already wafting about the place. The stage was set, with minimal lighting, strategically-placed candles, and a pile of electronics and winking lights straight out of *Forbidden Planet.* The music emanating from the pile of Moog Modulars started in meditative mode with Mellotrons to the fore. The acoustic in Liverpool Cathedral has a notoriously long reverb, and sounds are inclined to swirl about; the group seemed to take this into account, favouring the more washy end of the spectrum for much of the concert. That, combined with the quad sound, enhanced the swirling of the music, to good effect. My memory

> tells me they also had an extra speaker up in the tower, so sounds came from all directions, but that may have been the 'exotic smoke' beginning to take its toll! From my perspective, the mesmeric pulse of the sequencers were what stayed in my memory the most – my recollection is that they were a bit more prominent in the mix than subsequent bootlegs might suggest. In any event, the sound of a Moog Modular in full flight through a decent PA, was a new thing at that time – and to me, the sound was overwhelming in its richness and power. The entire audience seemed to go into a collective trance, hypnotised by the stately progression of small red lights dancing across the sequencers in time to the pulse. Tangerine Dream were on top form, and that collective magic that happens when a group of like-minded musicians hit their stride, was in full flow. When the concert finally ended to rapturous applause, many of the audience seemed dazed as they emerged blinking into the night – with one or two having difficulty finding the door! I think everyone present realised they had witnessed something special which would last in the memory for a long time.

Another significant concert and venue was Coventry Cathedral, filmed by Tony Palmer. (The Manor Mobile also recorded the whole Coventry gig, but only the first set was archived and preserved, later to be included in the *In Search of Hades* box set.) Over the years the truth about this concert has become distorted. Acclaimed musician Steve Dinsdale of the admired trio Radio Massacre International wrote to Tony Palmer some years ago and received a full reply. Here, Steve takes up the tale in a personal communication to me:

> All of this story is from Tony Palmer himself, via an email to me in about 2003. The whole concert was filmed by Palmer with original sound. He then made a 52-minute edit with the intention that it would be shown on the BBC TV *Omnibus* arts programme, still with original sound. It was sent to Virgin for approval, and it's here that things get murky. The next thing Palmer knew, the edit emerged in October 1976 as a standalone shown on BBC 2 on a Sunday night at 8.15 p.m., re-edited to 30 minutes and with *Ricochet* dubbed as the soundtrack, together with a caption at the end: 'Music from the album *Ricochet* on Virgin Records' (or words to that effect). Palmer knew nothing about this, having delivered his edit with original sound, and presumably having been paid. It seems likely to me that Virgin saw the opportunity to turn it into a cheeky advert for

> one of their products (Pretty audacious, seeing as advertising was strictly banned on the BBC). It could also be the case that maybe they didn't think the concert music was very representative of Tangerine Dream, at least for new listeners, and decided that *Ricochet* was more appropriate. In the process, they reduced a film of what was a very special event, down to a farce with none of the original concert sound. Personally, I've seen the pictures so many times, I never really need to see them again, but the original audio is an absolute treasure, and it's this which should be cherished. The group normally played in the dark at this time anyway so that people would concentrate on the music, and that's what people should do with this, I think! All subsequent enquiries from Palmer fell on stony ground.

As a coda, Steve added the following remark: 'On *In Search Of Hades*, the TV showing is somehow attributed as being an *Old Grey Whistle Test* special. This isn't true. It was simply billed *Tangerine Dream at Coventry Cathedral*'. Peter Baumann remembered this particular concert in his 2020 musicradar.com interview:

> Nothing was planned. We were asked to play a concert in a cathedral, and we thought, 'Yeah, that sounds like a great idea'. The acoustics weren't always so good, but the atmosphere was incredible. A cathedral or a church is an excellent place to listen to music, because you walk inside and you immediately feel calm ... Your awareness is expanded. That was perfect for listening to Tangerine Dream.

The British gig schedule led to the live album *Ricochet*, released at the very end of the year. However, this LP was only live in the sense that side B was a concert recording. Side A was put together from sections, including from the acclaimed Croydon Fairfield Halls concert of 23 October. It was only with the release of *Bootleg Box Set Volume 1* that fans knew firsthand how *Ricochet* had been stitched together; only fan-circulated tapes had previously given the game away.

Ricochet (1975)

Personnel:

Edgar Froese: keyboards, synths, guitar

Chris Franke: keyboards, synths, drums

Peter Baumann: keyboards, synths

Producer: Tangerine Dream and Chris Blake
Recorded at the Manor, Oxfordshire: October 1975
Release date: UK and US: December 1975
Chart placings: UK: 40
Running time: 38:15
Side One: 1. 'Ricochet, Part One' (Tangerine Dream)
Side Two: 1. 'Ricochet, Part Two' (Tangerine Dream)

Presented in two side-long parts, the first part – though using musical material from the band's famed date at Croydon Fairfield Halls on 23 October 1975 – is in fact a studio creation put together from a selection of improvised sessions. However, the piece opens with audience noise and applause, giving the listener the impression of being at a gig. A chiming synth opens the track, dramatic single notes sounding out before a white noise rhythm and sequence start. Whirring synths accompany this section, adding to the drama – something is going to *happen,* a common evocation in the band's early music – before the first improvised section begins. Rolling chords are added to this three-note sequence until Froese's guitar adds a distinctive riff, augmented with a synth harmony, which itself develops as the section continues, along with synth chords and new melodies. This tone of light and melody makes a striking change from the pieces on the previous two albums, new percussion, cymbals and Mellotron-brass harmonies, making this music more dramatic. There is a sense of opening out from a simple seed, of musical flowering, as each new synth line, chord and augmented harmony adds to the music.

After six minutes, when all the harmonies are different – though the underlying music remains the same – a weirdly delayed German voice bursts into the mix, speaking incomprehensibly and acting as a bridge to the next section, which, though new, relates musically to the first section. This second section begins with more filtered white noise and synth bleeps, before turning into a new sequence and set of chords, much faster in tempo than anything before. Here, Franke's precision sequencing comes to the fore, as he pulls individual notes out of the 5/4 sequence, accompanied by a whirring chord and Froese's guitar feedback. The mood is one of chase, flight and pursuit – not unlike Pink Floyd's 'On The Run', which this section is similar to. But then the Tangerine Dream melodies and harmonies return, giving the piece much more of a light, melodious tone, and relating it to the first sonic excursion. Synth solos also lighten the mood, taking the listener's attention away, then returning it, as the shimmering, oscillating white noise and Moog notes echo and vibrate.

As the guitar returns and more chords and solo lines are piled onto the mix, the piece comes to a dramatic conclusion, the sequence returning to a 4/4 time signature, acquiring drums, percussion and yet more harmonies, before heading off into another bridge, this time constructed from drones and the echoed, reverberated remains of rhythmic patterns and guitar feedback. Now the drone is the same timbre as the opening chimes, returning the piece to its musical origin. It is a tranquil conclusion to a breathless journey, one constructed in the main from Chris Franke's brilliant sequencer work.

Side B opens – in the original version – with what sounds like a couple of claps from an audience member, and in fact this is what it is, left on the front of the tape. This side was created from a genuine recording of the Fairfield Halls concert, opening with one of the most famous Tangerine Dream moments – a simple, beautiful piano melody, albeit played by Froese on a grand piano at the Manor. As Wouter Bessels revealed in the book accompanying the *In Search Of Hades* set, about eight minutes of side B is taken from the Croydon gig, a fact known from the session sheets included with the multi-track tapes.

The piece is in two parts, the first starting with Mellotrons and a more melodically and harmonically sophisticated version of the piano, before the Mellotrons head off into inner space on their own. After this, a light, high-register sequence begins, changing from moment to moment like a flock of birds on the wing, before deeper sequencer notes emerge, then more Mellotrons, including the brass – this also bringing in a new theme. The trio are very much doing what they do best here, with a glorious combination of rippling sequencers, Mellotrons and synths; changing, transmuting, taking the listener on a sonic flight. This first part has a wonderful aerial quality to it, as if, from high up, the listener can see huge vistas all around.

As the sequencer becomes more urgent, new synths arrive – these more squealing in tone, adding a dramatic layer, until they are at the fore of the music alongside dozens of rippling notes. Then white noise percussion arrives, and a new layer of backing chords, a dense structure emerging based on the original theme yet far more elemental in timbre. When a further set of chords comes in with a silky string synth, the listener is cast upon a linear journey, *from* somewhere *to* somewhere, carried by propulsive rhythms. Froese's electric guitar makes a new entrance alongside a mellow synth, these pair of lines – one oscillator-electric, one summoned from strings and amp feedback – vying with one another in a most thrilling way. Now the sequence is deep and simple, allowing musical headroom for the two leads, which continue to melodically challenge, support and complement one another. Played live on the night, this was one of the group's great moments.

Eventually, the sequencer changes rhythm and timbre as a new set of synth lines arrive, one of them developing an earlier melody. A new sequence ostinato also comes into play, adding a layer of harmony. White noise patterns mark the sequences as Froese's guitar returns to squalling feedback, and for a moment, the music's forward motion slows, as if taking a breath before the melodic theme re-emerges.

A sonic bridge takes the listener out of this frantic section: more Germanic voices, echoed and delayed, in a manner Michael Hoenig used later for his classic *Departure From The Northern Wastelands* album. Strange, otherworldly industrial noises counterpoint the human vocalisations, with a few synth effects thrown in for good measure, before the trusty Mellotron flutes carry the listener out of this weird sonic pit.

The second part of this side – also taken from the Croydon concert – opens with a solitary sequence, crystalline in timbre, before deeper notes and keyboard chords come in to augment it. The feel of this section matches the first, albeit with a different harmonic structure. The tempo and overall mood, however, is clearly the same as the first piece, though the tone is lighter. A wonderful synth solo climbs over this sequence before the ostinato structure steadies and returns to four beats to the bar.

The music now has an aura of conclusion. The sequences take on new patterns as Franke uses the adaptive method to transmute ostinatos, before the synth solo – now quieter – returns one last time. As the piece ends, a sonorous string synth harmonises with the original set of sequencer notes before fading into audio distance, as a final, doomy, low-register chord emerges. The pace has dropped: the tone is elegiac. A Mellotron choir sets up the piece's ending, and then the audience bursts into applause.

With *Ricochet* being beloved of fans – even after the discovery on the *Bootleg Box Set Volume 1* that the untampered-with and complete Fairfield Halls recording proved side one was a studio lash-up – what little damage was done did nothing to diminish enthusiasm for the album. Frequently cited as a fan favourite, *Ricochet* captures the groundbreaking musical achievements of Franke in particular, whose style of adaptive live Moog-playing – albeit based on memorised sequences – laid the foundation for all Berlin School music to follow.

Franke remarked on this album in the group's 1986 interview with Johnny Black in issue 17 of *thisBEAT*:

> *Ricochet* is probably my favourite because it proved that when we create live music, it is always different. When we create in the studio, we pursue particular directions and we experiment, and it becomes more polished; but somehow, the live-work remains more classic. *Ricochet* still says something to me.

As was often the case, Froese's wife Monique provided the front cover image: a photograph she took at the Bordeaux seaside.

But even two classic releases was not enough for Froese. Enthused by the recording of and response to his debut solo LP *Aqua*, in June and July he recorded the music that would appear as his second solo album *Epsilon In Malaysian Pale*. This album is much admired for its Mellotron, and stands as a tribute not only to Froese's energy and ability to manage his artistic and touring schedule, but to how he followed his artistic muse. First released on Virgin Records, a second identical issue (titled *Ypsilon In Malaysian Pale)* came out on Brain Records, famous for releasing Klaus Schulze's classic albums amongst many others. The LP's front cover artwork was greatly influenced by Froese's experiences touring Australia with the group, the ferns, in all their sumptuous green, evoking that experience.

1976 – Gigs, Gear, Arguments

The first half of the year was taken up by European dates, including Germany, France and Spain in January, Belgium and Netherlands in February, and various gigs in Britain and Germany over the summer. Some of these gigs turned out to be classics that were later released in various forms – the Pabellon de la Casilla concert in Bilbao: released in the *Bootleg Box Set Volume 1* for instance; or the 27 June gig at the so-called Berlin Philharmonics, which also appeared in the 'orange box' (*Bootleg Box Set*).

In June at Berlin's Amber Studios, Froese took time to record the music for his third solo album *Macula Transfer*, the LP appearing at the end of the month on Brain Records. (In later years, this album would be dogged by legal issues, leading Froese in due course to re-record and augment the original music in order to avoid copyright issues.) The music was all composed during the tour undertaken earlier in the year, with Froese working on the material during plane flights. Each of the five tracks, therefore, carried a flight reference as its title: 'OS 452', 'AF 765', 'PA 701', 'Qantas 611' and 'IF 810'. The music was not as inspired as his first two LPs, lacking some of their bite and originality, and featuring a rather limp guitar solo, though the latter tracks are much better than the opening ones.

Around the same time Baumann recorded his first solo album *Romance 76* – a work unlike anything the group had done, though, in places, its A-side recalled some of the timbres of *Stratosfear*. Much of the B-side was sparse, albeit augmented with an orchestra, a situation in part influenced by David Bowie's comments on the music – Bowie was in his Berlin phase at the time. But Baumann was beginning to struggle with his place in Tangerine Dream, and this in time would lead to his departure. The solo album, though, was well-received and managed to court some radio play. Baumann was zealous in his promotion of it.

Bowie knew Froese too, and the pair often discussed music. In an interview given to *NME* in July 1977, Froese recalled their friendship: 'He got a flat in Berlin, and every day or every second day we went out and had long conversations about art – techniques and the styles of painting. But the problem was that my time plan was different from his time plan'. At various points from May to September, however, the group worked on a project that would in time be of enormous significance to Tangerine Dream, since it signposted the way to what would become their highly successful film soundtrack career. William Friedkin needed music for his film *Sorcerer*, and having seen Tangerine Dream playing, he enthusiastically courted them. This resulted in a wonderfully atmospheric album, which all three musicians contributed to and played on.

Sorcerer (1977)

Personnel:
Edgar Froese: Twin-keyboard Mellotron Mark V, Steinway grand piano, Oberheim polyphonic, ARP Omni, PPG, modified Moog, electric guitars
Chris Franke: Moog Modular, Projekt Elektronik sequencer, Computerstudio Digital Sequencer, Mellotron, ARP Pro Soloist, Elka String synthesizer, Oberheim sequencer
Peter Baumann: Projekt Elektronik modular synthesizer, Projekt Elektronik sequencer, Fender Rhodes, ARP Pro Soloist, Mellotron.
Producer: Tangerine Dream
Recorded at Victoria Studios, Berlin: May-October 1976
Release date: UK and US: July 1977
Chart placings: UK: 25
Running time: 43:52
All tracks by Tangerine Dream
Side One: 1. 'Main Title' 2. 'Search' 3. 'The Call' 4. 'Creation' 5. 'Vengeance' 6. 'The Journey' Side Two: 1. 'Grind' 2. 'Rain Forest' 3. 'The Abyss' 4. 'The Mountain Road' 5. 'Impressions Of Sorcerer' 6. 'Betrayal (Sorcerer Theme)'

Sorcerer was the first of what would be many Tangerine Dream soundtracks. William Friedkin's 1977 film was considered by most – though not by its director – to be a remake of the 1953 film *The Wages Of Fear*. *Sorcerer* the film was not well received by critics, though the Tangerine Dream soundtrack was, and as a classic of 1970s synth work, it deserved those plaudits. But the relationship between director and band was unusual, in that Friedkin asked Froese to write music based only on the script; Froese saw none of the film roughs. After Froese delivered a complete score to Friedkin, the director then used the music to edit the film to, reversing the usual way of working. Froese later made a wry comment about the soundtrack being his most uncomplicated experience of working with Hollywood.

Opening with the main title theme, a thrumming synth sets the music in motion, to which whooshing effects are added. The synth changes pitch then performs a deep glissando down, then up again, as the eerie keyboard effects multiply and cascade around the mix. More white noise synths appear, before a wispy keyboard brings a hint of melody, albeit accompanied by whirring, gothic synths, which in due course dominate the mix. This track is reminiscent in tone and mood of *Phaedra* from three years earlier.

'Search' is a traditional sequenced piece, here accompanied by Mellotron strings taking up the melodic theme. Only three minutes long, it manages to convey a sense of impending action through its later use of the Mellotron brass. A subtle synth lead takes up the melody as the sequences change from 4/4 to 2/4 and back to 4/4 again, in a hint of the compositions used on *Stratosfear*.

With 'The Call', however, the mood is lighter, the tempo slower, the main focus a chiming backdrop over which a Mellotron theme plays, harmonised later with a swooping synth. It is another effective atmospheric piece.

'Creation' dials the vibe down further – dark, ambient synth washes drifting this way and that, apparently at random... until a *Stratosfear*-style sequence emerges, and with it a synth solo. The mood is dark but not macabre; subtle guitar adds texture. This is sonics describing *tension*, not fear. The solos are light with plenty of space, and the accompaniment is minimal. Most of the supporting notes are short, with much left in the musical description for space and reverb. Another moody piece, perfectly judged.

'Vengeance' is based on a loping, staccato rhythm, to which a bassy resonant synth is added, then a lighter, more ethereal one. When the key changes, however, new synths enter the mix, adding tension, though this swiftly subsides. When this key change happens again cymbals crash, marking twists and turns, and as the music develops to its conclusion the synths never let up, adding even more of a sense of impending disaster. By the end of the cut, all the listener can hear is those persistent, overwhelming chords, with just whistling effects and a hint of a synth lead to pull them out of the sonic pit.

'The Journey' opens with a marvellously funky keyboard riff thrumming away (it is actually a sequence), over which other synths jostle for space. Soon though, a lead Mellotron flute sounds out, indicating the possibility of a journey. As the funky synth chugs away, the flute pairs with other synths to evoke travel. Too short a track, alas!

With 'Grind', however, we are back in traditional Berlin School territory, the Mellotron brass and a chiming synth to the fore over a classic echoed sequence. A bridge over descending chords adds musical variety before a dense, dark piano emerges for just a few moments. Then it is back to Mellotron and synth, this time with some harmonic variation over slightly transmuted chords. The Mellotron work here is particularly good, especially as the delay opens out, giving the sequences a bit more movement.

'Rain Forest' is another sequence-based piece, but by virtue of its twisted effects and bouncing ostinato it is a particularly effective evocation of environment. Electronic instruments evoke strange frogs and insects, while the melodic material is as twisted as anything else on the soundtrack, the whirring, emotionally charged chords rising and falling in unexpected, almost atonal modes. Nothing sounds stable. Nothing sounds European.

In 'Abyss', the group create a dark, charged atmosphere, using bass synths, whirring, woozy effects, the Mellotron cello (rarely used) and various other synth effects. This really is music for the pit – the listener is right on the edge, with the insistent looping Mellotron cello the signifier, evoking a sense of imbalance at the rim of the abyss itself. When this loop speeds up a little and new effects enter the mix, there is almost imbalance, but the music fades, to be replaced with glissando pitch shifts and atonal synth washes: the effluvia of the abyss rising up to intoxicate and defeat the senses. All of a sudden, a sequence emerges in a major key: light in the darkness. More sequences bubble up as the listener is transported over the abyss, rising, carried by new waves of music. At the end, mystery suffuses everything as the sequences go mad, changing pitch without rhyme or reason, until, at their climax, they cut off in a wash of Mellotron chords and crazy phasing. This track is the highlight of the whole album, brilliantly composed and arranged.

In contrast, 'The Mountain Road' evokes something more esoteric – peaks and valleys, here described with simple chords and a staccato sequence riff, which in places sounds more like orchestral percussion. The Mellotron flutes come to the fore as Baumann's Fender Rhodes chords support the music, again evoking uplands.

'Impressions Of Sorcerer' is another light sequenced piece, this time reverting to Mellotron brass and airy synths, with Froese's guitar supplying a more earthy, terrestrial tone. There is even a hint of funk in the choppy guitar chords and curtailed notes of the sequence, which in due course is overlaid by the main melodic theme and a pair of strident Mellotron brass chords. As the piece concludes, the solo flies high, a frisson of white noise percussion accompanying it.

'Betrayal', the theme of *Sorcerer*, is another strong composition, given drive and energy by using just two notes in the main sequence, a high-resonance filter adding synth drama. The main theme is delivered with the Mellotron strings, a wailing synth lead counterpointing in places. The use of filtered high-resonance synth sounds is particularly effective here.

All in all, this first soundtrack – recorded in 1976 but not released until summer 1977 – was a complete album in itself, composed with little formal reference to the film visuals, therefore taking on its own mood and timbre. No wonder Friedkin was so pleased with it. Enamoured of the band after seeing them in concert, he knew quality when he heard it. This soundtrack was his proof.

By now, the group needed a new studio album, so in August they decamped to Audio Studios in Berlin, where they proceeded to record what became *Stratosfear*.

From the start there were technical difficulties. Baumann was using his brand new Projekt Electronik rhythm computer, which gave the album's percussive sequences their characteristically dry and precise timbre. This device, however, had taken the German manufacturer a long time to make, and in the studio it proved unreliable, at one point its recorders breaking down, with smoke pouring out of the Dolby noise-reduction units. There were also interpersonal issues, the trio arguing over which tracks should be worked on in order to make it to the finished LP.

In his interview given to Mark Prendergast for the 1994 box set *Tangents*, Froese recalled the situation at Audio Studios:

> When I appeared in the studio one day with a harmonica, the absurdity of the situation was revealed. It was supposed to be a joke retort to the unpredictability of the technology, but after playing it during the beginning of '3 AM At The Border Of The Marsh From Okefenokee', everybody decided to leave it on. So much had happened during these sessions – master tapes at times disappeared from the studio; finished tracks were mysteriously erased, and the mixing console finally went up in smoke.

In the group's April 1986 interview for *thisBeat,* Franke also remembered those days:

> Normally when we go into the studio, there's no music written, and we work by a system of trial and error. We work like Salvador Dali, so we're more like developers than composers ... we play little bits, record them on tape or in the computer, decide immediately if we want to keep them

> or change them. It's a kind of composition that could not have happened before, because you would need an orchestra to be playing all the parts.

But for all its difficulties, the album would go down in group lore as one of their very best, characterised by its emphasis on melody, acoustic instruments – in particular Froese's guitar – and a kind of light, almost somnolent feel, which contrasted with the heavy forbidding atmosphere of *Rubycon*, recorded only a year and a half earlier.

Stratosfear (1976)

Personnel:
Edgar Froese: Moog, Mellotron, guitars, grand piano, bass, harmonica
Chris Franke: Moog, organ, percussion, Mellotron, harpsichord
Peter Baumann: Moog, Projekt Elektronik rhythm computer, Fender Rhodes, Mellotron
Producer: Tangerine Dream and Ottmar Bergler
Recorded at Audio Studio, Berlin: August 1976
Release dates: UK and US: October 1976
Chart placings: UK: 39
Running time: 35:39
All tracks by Tangerine Dream
Side One: 1. 'Stratosfear' 2. 'The Big Sleep In Search Of Hades'
Side Two: 1. '3 AM At The Border Of The Marsh From Okefenokee' 2. 'Invisible Limits'

Stratosfear marked a change in the band's direction, from dense improvised pieces with spacey settings to more structured and melodic tracks – often short, or at least shorter than previous side-long epics. The album had four such pieces, beginning with the title track, which opens with soft, sustained chords against which a guitar arpeggio ripples. Almost at once, a simple sequence emerges, providing the backing for a melody and a chord sequence. The composition's direct, natural quality is apparent at once – recognisably Tangerine Dream, yet somehow invested with a bucolic, almost sunny mood. As the piece progresses, the sequences transform a little and harmonic augmentation is added; also a soaring solo synth line. Double-tempo sequences and a new set of guitar chords counterpoint a second melodic theme, before the music heads off again into solo synth textures.

As the music breaks down, a new melody emerges, Froese chopping out guitar chords which the keyboard mimics. As heavier percussive elements arrive, the synths again change timbre, keeping to the ascending-note melody while adding tonal flourishes. A second sequencer and guitar bridge leads to a variation on the theme, then to a much heavier sequenced section. Already there is a great deal of movement in the piece, both subtle and obvious, rhythmically and melodically. When the original theme returns, the mood becomes more restrained, albeit again with a soaring synth in counterpoint.

Now a half-speed rhythm takes over, with new solos and new white noise percussion. Harmonies fly in all directions as an earlier melody reappears, then more thrumming drums, working the piece into a dramatic section, before a classic Froese guitar solo enters the mix: effects swiftly degrading it into feedback, echo and reverb. Now the mood becomes calm, as a synth solo comes to the fore. The music fades. Near silence... then the opening guitar chords and arpeggio return, underpinned by a new chord sequence, adding further harmonic invention to this already busy piece. By the end, many variations have passed, and all in little more than ten minutes: a far cry from the dense epics of *Rubycon*.

The second piece, 'The Big Sleep In Search Of Hades' opens with a beautiful melody – no introduction, just straight in, with Froese's guitar arpeggios in accompaniment, and even a bass guitar. Again tapping into a bucolic mood of sunlit warmth, the piece goes through several variations, including an eerie, woozy bridge with a Mellotron strings chord underpinning it: the dream after the siesta perhaps. Soft, simple synth lines bounce around; then a weird Mellotron choir appears – a hint of a dream again – before the melodic theme emerges once more.

As a new synth plays out a novel melodic line, a thrumming bass note underpins the music, accompanied by more Mellotrons... and then it is back to the original melody. Dream has returned to sleep. What is particularly noticeable in this short track is the band's confidence in using their melodic material: a step forwards and a step sideways simultaneously.

Side B opens with '3 AM At The Border Of The Marsh From Okefenokee', which features that most un-Tangerine-Dream of instruments, the harmonica. But good use is made of it, as an evocative, possibly nocturnal, possibly dreamlike scene is described with melody and sparse instrumentation. Yet it is terrifically effective; subtle and simple at the same time. The band even seem to be looking west, as the track's title and the harmonica hint at America. After this introduction, rippling burbles arrive like synthesized cicadas. Then a filtered synth line and a wonderfully dense, ascending gothic chord – which thickens, sharpens and rises to a sudden crescendo – fade into a Mellotron choir.

Now a new sequence begins, with its own melody and chord structure. As the rhythm doubles, the Mellotron flutes so beloved of Froese enter the mix, adding a melodic lead line which a second sequence then counterpoints. Other keyboards bring new melodies – including a twinkling Rhodes – transmuting into lead lines, as further sequenced elements rise and fall. The mood is one of light sleep, slumber without dream – safe, peaceful, tranquil. In some ways, this whole album is about sleep and dream.

As the Mellotron flutes return, a sound like electronic sheep emerges as if from nearby pastures, alongside, in the final moments, the return of the harmonica. Again, the bucolic element is strong – quiet, on a vast scale, yet safe and at peace. It is a wonderful evocation of a western night, perhaps in the American Southwest, with all its various moods and strands.

The last track, 'Invisible Limits,' opens with another simple sequence, a wash of undistorted guitar chords its counterpoint. This time the melody is in the sequence alone, altered by underlying chord changes. The Mellotron flutes are high in the mix, linking this music with all that has gone before. Again, the atmosphere is restful: night, or dawn at the latest.

As two key changes in the sequence alter the piece's structure, new chords anchor the work, Froese's guitar adding wah-wah dimensions before a sudden drum attack announces something different approaching, then a bell and a great chord, sustained...

Whatever was on its way is now *here,* conveyed by Froese's guitar line and a synth harmony. But we do not know what it *is* that's here, not least because it departs so soon, leaving something akin to yet different from the Tangerine Dream classics of old – a new guitar solo, a new guitar sound, then a sudden change to double-speed, oscillating and rippling...

Now Froese's guitar solo takes the lead, riding the music in bluesy style. After a while, a brand-new melody arrives, as the music becomes more urgent, drama coming from the synth and the quick-tempo sequence, which follows the chord structure moment by moment. After a synth bridge and a key change, Froese unleashes another wonderful guitar solo – so unexpected, yet beautifully arranged... sparse, melodic. But then, as synth burbles rise, a new, atonal chord emerges and the guitar fades; dream or nightmare, we do not know. The newly-arrived thing has gone already, and what is left is a hint of the old guitar and twinkling sonic dust – and then a great, empty, silent space. We can hear its extent in the reverberation's immensity.

This piece, like all on the album, is marked by confidence of musicality, melodic invention and subtlety of harmony. As its synth twinkles fade, a simple piano emerges, taking a 3/4 rhythm and a melody against which chords are added: a coda, a definite musical statement, a strong, solid ending. It is as if a decision has been taken for the new morning. Soon, the Mellotron flutes add a harmony, and then, not long after it began, the coda is over, ending in the crash of a single piano chord.

Night has passed. It is morning now: daylight.

For all its eventual beauty, light and wonder, mixing the recorded music proved to be difficult. The first mix was handed over to Pink Floyd's Nick Mason, who was working at the Hansa Tonstudio in Berlin. But because of a dispute between Virgin and the band, that mix was shelved. In 1994, for *Tangents,* Froese recalled recording *Stratosfear,* saying, 'The events which occurred during the making of *Stratosfear* alone, would fill an entire book!'

The album was released in October, eventually being certified with silver status. The group went on an extensive second European tour to promote it, with dates in Germany, Britain, Belgium, Spain and France. One of these gigs – the Albert Hall Nottingham date of 8 November – made it to the *Bootleg Box Set Volume 2*.

Electronic music fan and British EM promoter Dave Buxton recalled events in Nottingham that year:

> My first Tangerine Dream concert took place when I was a teenager. I did not go to gigs much at this time, having no transport, so a chance to see Tangerine Dream locally – only a bus ride into Nottingham – was too much of an opportunity to miss ... The lineup was Froese, Franke and Baumann. I remember marvelling at the setup in place in front of the Albert Hall pipe organ before the start of the gig as we took our seats in the balcony, stage-right of the band. It was Chris Franke's telephone-exchange-of-a-rig that really caught our eye – dominating the stage behind the other two rigs like some mad professor's invention with many pulsating flashing lights and the odd keyboard, it took one's breath away. My memory of what they played is vivid, as I'd recently bought the album: it was *Stratosfear* ... As we watched from the balcony, we noticed a large silver disco ball in the

centre of the venue start to vibrate. As the music got louder, the disco ball started to actually shake. We wondered if it would survive the crescendo of sound, or fall, but fortunately, it was firmly secured and survived the vibrations, and the concert continued. I loved the extended piece, as I was a little disappointed that they were playing mostly composed music: I had hoped for a complete improvised performance. Still, it was a great gig, and both the title track 'Stratosfear' and 'Invisible Limits' were outstanding. I can't remember whether they played an encore or not, but I have a feeling they did: another improvised piece.

Electronic music fan Alan Walker also saw the group on this tour:

I was sixteen and this was, I think, my first major gig. I was a big Tangerine Dream enthusiast, picking up the fantastic mesmeric qualities of their music on *Ricochet*, and that they were true pioneers, taking big synth sounds into the rock mainstream. I was a little disappointed with the new direction the group were heading with *Stratosfear*, preferring the gloomy reflective predecessors: *Zeit* being and remaining one of my all-time favourite albums. That said, the gig was a fantastic journey into space for my then self, developing my musical taste. I remember the classic step-sequencer-driven head charges, well cranked to the max, ten minutes in, the guitar overlays, the big wardrobe synth cabinets. The gig is available to listen to ... on YouTube, and in writing this piece, it's the first time I have listened to it. Somewhere in the clapping is me, captured in the moment, frozen in time, spotty and awed. So for me, Tangerine Dream are an evocation of my own past as much as a musical experience. As a stroppy young obscurist, they were a good leg up the credibility ladder for me, especially boggling minds over the speakers in the school common room where Fleetwood Mac and Eagles were the norm...

Another lucky gig attendee was David Elliott of *Neumusik* fanzine, who saw the group in Portsmouth on 9 November:

I'm fifteen, it's a school weekday and I'm off to Portsmouth to see Tangerine Dream for the first time – a short train ride away from my hometown of Chichester (where I'd almost seen them two years earlier, but that's another story). I already have several albums, but the anticipation of seeing this impossibly mysterious group is like going on a first date. It's less like they're from Germany; more like the far reaches of the solar system – it's more like they're monitoring the insertion of uranium rods into an atomic pile, than creating music. Brought up on rock's standard guitar/bass/drums, it cannot be overstated how mind-shifting it is to see those three big blocks of electronic machinery. So, music can be performed like this and sound like this? It is still *rock* in the sense that it's very loud, there's a groove and Froese does get up and play his guitar. That's the bit I like least. As a different sound source, fine, but a wailing solo seems somehow out of place. The groove, however, is irresistible. When the sequencers come in – with their rich tones, interweaving, sometimes clattering counter-rhythms and offbeats – I want it to last forever. It's also highly melodic: a fact often omitted from reviews. There are references to 'Stratosfear', but mostly it's improvised. The whole concert is on YouTube now and listening back to it 45 years later, it sounds better – more strident than the somewhat underwhelming *Encore* which was compiled from the US leg of the tour. I saw them a year and a half later, again in Portsmouth, on the Cyclone tour, but by then, Baumann had left, replaced (albeit briefly) by a drummer and vocalist. So glad I saw them in their prime.

1977 – Arguments, America, Development

The opening months of the year were taken up with preparations for the group's North American tour. Dates were set for 29 March to 26 April. This was a highly successful tour, with a great deal of recording going on, at soundchecks, rehearsals, plus the concerts themselves. American audiences were enthusiastic, as were the radio presenters lucky enough to broadcast the music – the former showing their appreciation via whoops which would in due course make it to vinyl, the latter in some cases whispering and speaking over the music in their desire to be part of the event (e.g., the presenter from Montreal's CHOM FM, who clearly had a fantastic time listening to the gig).

These dates led in due course to the group's second live album *Encore.* At the time, the LP stated it was 'Recorded live during March/April 1977'. But in fact, like *Ricochet*, the double LP was a bit of a lash-up, created in the main by Baumann, for whom the work was to mark an ending.

Baumann has commented in various places about his departure from the group. In his 2020 musicradar.com interview, he described his feelings at the time: 'We put out some great albums and had some amazing success, but it began to feel like work. When we started, there were no rules. It was just about having fun and making music. Then it became a job. I wanted to try something different'.

In the group's interview for *Prog* magazine, Baumann and Froese both gave their opinions on events. Baumann was sanguine: 'When you've had a good run, you sense that it's coming to some sort of end. It just felt like it wasn't as much fun anymore. And I think Edgar wanted to go in some other direction'.

Froese had a different perspective on that time: 'I had to ask Peter Baumann to leave the band after he had performed a very offensive and egocentric affair about developing his solo career after our two US tours in 1977. Also, my relationship with Christopher Franke was quite strained'.

Froese also spoke to David Elliott in *Neumusik* about that tumultuous time:

> We booked the studio for January 1978 ... and four months before that, I told Peter Baumann to leave the band. We were in a grave situation stylistically. We wanted to go on further, creating new things and buying

> more equipment, learning a lot of new stuff. With his studio, he couldn't even practice with us because his studio was taking up all his time.

Froese was asked if there was there any aggression involved:

> No aggression, but it was a little strange during the American tour when he (Baumann) said, 'Right, I have to go back to Berlin for a few days to see a guy who is doing the acoustics in the studio'. It's not on. But anyway, we didn't split on a fight. We just told him to leave, and in the end, I think he felt okay with us. He's gone to America now, and in the meantime, he's sold his studio and is setting up a new one in New York. It's stupid, and he's done it for nothing really. He ... is now sitting in a room somewhere, playing some sort of music. Still, if he feels okay, then that's alright.

But Baumann was possibly not in the best headspace in 1977. Speaking to *Musikexpress* in November of that year, he gave an indication of his feelings for his native country:

> There was a time when certain German groups and solo artists were quite interesting, but in some way, they did not develop that further. I don't know if the fault lies with the record companies or the audience ... For me, Germany is basically a very depressive country – I believe that this negative attitude in the whole of society is always subliminally understood. This is really my pet hate: no real enthusiasm, no real lust for life!

Baumann, however, did a terrific job putting together the live album from the mass of recordings available to him. Even after the truth of its creation was revealed, it still stood up as a wonderful listen and a great record of the atmosphere of those first American and Canadian gigs. The group went back to North America in the summer, but the promotion company folded and only four dates were played. *Encore,* though, did contain one almost-untouched live recording – 'Monolight' – which was taken almost in its entirety from the 4 April Lisner Auditorium gig in Washington D.C. A new, fuller version was presented in the *Bootleg Box Set Volume 2* blue box. Two other dates from this tour also received formal releases long after: Ford Auditorium, Detroit from 31 March, as part of the *Bootmon* series, and 9 April at Place des

Arts, Montreal, also part of the *Bootmon* series; the gig recorded and broadcast by CHOM FM.

Encore (1977)

Personnel:
Edgar Froese: electric guitar, Steinway Grand Piano, ARP Omni, Mellotron V, Moog Modular, Oberheim Four Voice, Palm Products GmbH 1020, Projekt Elektronik sequencer
Chris Franke: ARP Pro Soloist, ELKA Rhapsody 610, Mellotron M400, Moog Modular, Oberheim OB-1, electronic percussion, Projekt Elektronik sequencer, Computerstudio digital sequencer, Oberheim sequencer
Peter Baumann: Fender Rhodes, ARP Pro Soloist, ELKA Rhapsody 610, EMS Vocoder, Mellotron M400, Projekt Elektronik Modular, Projekt Elektronik sequencer
Producer: Tangerine Dream
Recorded at various venues: spring 1977
Release date: UK and US: October 1977
Chart placings: UK: 55
Running time: 71:49
All tracks by Tangerine Dream
Side One: 1. 'Cherokee Lane'
Side Two: 1. 'Monolight'
Side Three: 1. 'Coldwater Canyon'
Side Four: 1. 'Desert Dream'

Early in 1977, Tangerine Dream undertook a successful American and Canadian tour, of which this album is the glorious document. A double-vinyl release, its four side-long tracks encompass the full range of their music, from shimmering sequenced pieces to more studied, melodic affairs, via studio lash-ups concocted from previously recorded but unused material.

The opening track 'Cherokee Lane' is emblematic of the trio's confidence. To a chorus of whoops and cheers, a deep, dense chord sounds out, heavily phased, veering off into novel oscillations as new layers and squealing sounds emerge. As these layers bleep and pulse, the mood lightens a little, before Mellotron strings chords begin, enunciating an off-kilter melody: sometimes major key, sometimes minor. Then a high-register two-note sequence begins, swiftly transmuting in rhythm and time signature as the music unfurls. The Mellotron strings match this sequence perfectly, and a little audience noise enlivens the proceedings.

As the sequence gains a bass register and goes into 5/4 time, the mood changes, acquiring drama and tension as various new elements compete in the mix – harmony synths, new Mellotron flute chords and melodic lines – and all to the enthusiastic noise of the audience. Baumann varies the rhythmic structure of the sequences a lot in this section, using his Projekt Elektronik sequencer (he often favoured a low bass line in unison with a high tinkling sequence four or more octaves above it), sometimes straight 4/4, elsewhere not. As two main lead lines surge this way and that, a distinct melodic pattern emerges, in harmony with the second keyboard. This is the sound of a group at the top of their game, improvising with extraordinary confidence in their chosen style. A second still stronger melody then begins, again harmonising with an additional keyboard.

As the Mellotron sound reverts to strings, the harmonic content flattens a little, using the second melody as a source over essentially one chord. Above this, however, the main lead line soars and dives, brilliantly played, with a kind of free-form verve evoking the headlong rush of the music. Now the bass register returns in the sequence as it goes four to the bar – steady and true, acting as a base for the Mellotron, occasionally stepping out into 5/4, then 2/4. As white noise percussion is introduced the Mellotron fades, to be replaced by keyboard chords, the mood now diminishing, approaching its conclusion, evoked as usual by the Mellotron flutes.

As the audience shows its appreciation, the musical energy disperses, and when the sequence fades, the tempo slows a little, carried by the Mellotron. At the end, all that is left is cheering and a repeated three-note Mellotron phrase that in due course rises, follows a lead line, then ends. It is a classic Tangerine Dream piece, which the audience love.

It should be noted here that as it is commonly thought some sections of this album were recorded in soundchecks and rehearsals, the notion that the audience wildly applauded each development is also unlikely. Some well-researched commentators believe the LP's entire audience reaction was taken from the same concert and applied to all four sides. It is accepted that *Encore* is a studio lash-up, created in the main by Baumann as his parting gift to the group.

The second track, 'Monolight' opens with a quirky, bouncing piano piece, redolent of a child skipping at random across crooked pavements. In due course, it quietens, changing to something akin to the piano piece on 'Invisible Limits' from *Stratosfear*, before giving way to shimmering synth, Mellotron-flute chords and a bizarre chorus of braying, gothic synths and deeply reverberated chimes.

As filtered white noise percussion takes over, a marching drum rhythm emerges, and with it a clear, formal, melodic piece set to a distinctive chord sequence. The lead line takes the melody and augments it as the piece progresses; and we know this is live because towards the end, there is a mistake, amended moments later: quick thinking!

The second main section is a more recognisable improvised piece, set to a thrumming, throbbing sequence in a low register. Mellotron brass chords bring great drama at once, stabbing out as a synth augments the chords and makes melody of its own. The sequences meanwhile change and develop in classic mode: the heartbeat of the band. Now the Mellotron brass takes the lead, as new synths score a chordal backdrop. Elements of this combination would appear the following year in the form of Froese's solo album *Ages* and the band's classic cut 'Madrigal Meridian'. The track ends with deep synths and a return to the solo piano, now with a harmonising synth lead above the repeating four-chord sequence, which Froese had been using since the European tour of autumn 1976.

The third side 'Coldwater Canyon' focuses on a simple staccato rhythm, the piece a setting for one of Froese's extended guitar solos, which, via various phased effects, completes a woozy, half-awake/half-stoned journey from low notes to high, then back again. Later on, this solo acquires a staccato feel of its own as synth chords emerge to duel with it, and then a competitive, piercing synth solo. The track eventually breaks down into a bleeping cacophony of effects, massive phasing and a few odd synth murmurs, with an occasional melodic interlude passing by.

'Desert Dream' is different from the preceding tracks in that it was mostly compiled from previously recorded material, including the unreleased (until 2019) soundtrack for the play *Oedipus Tyrannus* (specifically 'Overture' and 'Zeus'), and material recorded by Baumann himself in 1977 – 'Haunted Heights' was also an outtake from these sessions. The mood is reflective, even cosmic, with gorgeous drifting synths backing subtle keyboard lines and high modulation leads. This beautifully judged piece of ambience mutates at length into something darker as a deep synth note intones its call, accompanied by harsher noises like the sounds of clashing gate mechanisms and electronic hounds. Menace and dread are here. Soon, however, that menace is challenged through the soothing sound of the Mellotron flutes, albeit in turn pushed aside by a slow, chiming sequence and a simple chord structure. Above this, the Mellotron continues.

As the piece coalesces around a couple of melodic lead lines and a repetitive single-note sequence, the mood returns to drifting cosmic ambience, hints of *Stratosfear* mutating it into something specifically American. Chord changes further transform the music, giving it movement.

When echoed synth burbles come into focus, the music disintegrates once again, as if unable to maintain stable structure: a dreamlike invention, in fact. If 'Cherokee Lane' was broad daylight, this is now night, with all that implies. As this phantasmagorical interlude ends, a new mood begins, set in softly-oscillating sequences and chiming synths; but then, without warning, the interlude breaks, replaced with a formal Mellotron brass playing a slow, stately melody over a new chord sequence. It is a melancholy yet reverential piece to end the whole set; something elegiac, though undeniably wholesome, even when it breaks down into echoed synth noise and drifting keyboards. At the very end of the album, all the listener is left with are vague impressions of what went before: ghostly Mellotron, reverberant chimes, delicate wisps of synth noise.

The night is done. The gig is over. What remains is dawn, here evoked by a descending synth lead and a twin-track sequence in little more than a minute... then audience appreciation as the final note rings out.

The reception to many of the North American concerts was enthusiastic. After the Avery Fisher Hall concert in New York on 5 April, *Cashbox* printed the following appreciation:

> Tangerine Dream made it obvious that they still owe a great deal to their conventional rock heritage: the emphasis is on the beat. Each piece settled into a steady throb of mesmerizing effect at the bottom of a full spectrum of sound. The audience, for its part, couldn't get enough, calling the group back for four encores. At a post-concert reception, Froese said he 'still couldn't believe it'.

July saw the release of the *Sorcerer* soundtrack, coming one month after the film's debut. *Encore* was released in the autumn. Summer and autumn for Froese, however, was largely taken up with the recording of the monumental solo double-LP *Ages,* the front cover of which was adorned with one of his best photographic portraits. Recorded at Amber Studios in Berlin, this album has long polarised fans, some (like me) loving it, others put off by the 'simple' use of melody, and short tracks. Regardless of opinion, the album was a huge slab of electronica, notable in some regards for what was about to happen to the group.

In many ways, *Ages* was about progression. Both Froese and Franke were looking to put more structure into their music after four years of following the improvised or semi-improvised Berlin School formula. Change was in the air. With Baumann gone and the group reduced to a duo again – albeit with successful tours behind them, a global following and even a few commercially successful albums – they wanted both to move on musically and retain their fan base. Ironically, after *Ages,* the group released an album that would similarly split that fan base. *Ages* though was a wonderful set in itself, and remains a great listen to this day.

Of particular significance to the group was the appearance of drummer Klaus Krieger, who made his mark on Froese's fast-paced epic 'Nights Of Automatic Women'. Krieger would come to play a central role in what was to follow. He was an unusual drummer, manufacturing his own kits from plastic polymers, then thumping the life out of them. Froese invited him to record on one of the *Ages* cuts; the template of fast sequencing, synths and live drumming would prove momentous in the year that followed. The pair, however, were not the first to try this combination – Klaus Schulze pioneered its full use, working with human metronome Harald Grosskopf on his trailblazing epic 'Floating' from his album *Moondawn*. But 'Nights Of Automatic Women' was not only a superb track, it signposted the way ahead. 1978 was going to be a complicated year.

1978 – Development, Vocals, Progression

The new signpost had one direction on it: development. Froese and Franke felt the need to move on from lengthy Berlin School epics, wanting more structural focus in their music. With drummer Klaus Krieger on board, there was one more addition to make to the new group lineup.

Steve Jolliffe, born in England in 1949, was already a keen and gifted musician in his early adult life. In the late 1960s he played with Rick Davies in The Joint, before leaving to study music at the Berlin Konservatorium. Later, he chanced upon Froese, subsequently playing with Tangerine Dream before their first major successes. Later he joined Steamhammer – an early 1970s rock band – touring with them and contributing to the *Steamhammer II* album: including co-writing the French chart-topping single 'Autumn Song'. But it was in 1978 that both his and Tangerine Dream's stars properly collided. Writing to Froese to congratulate him on his musical success, Joliffe was surprised by a reply inviting him to make music with Froese, Franke and Krieger. What followed was to split the fan base and create one of the most surprising and debated albums of the group's career.

In January, *Ages* was released, and the quartet went into Berlin's Audio Studios to begin recording what would become *Cyclone.* Jolliffe was not only a flautist and reeds man; he could also sing. This led the way to two tracks featuring vocals – a first for the group, and something that took them into progressive territory. That year, progressive territory was already well-filled by Yes' *Tormato*, Genesis' *And Then There Were Three*, and Renaissance' *A Song For All Seasons* (the latter two bands scoring unexpected single-chart hits), but though punk was shaking up the music scene, Tangerine Dream were well-placed to add to the progressive *oeuvre*. And they did.

In the interview for this book, I spoke with Steve Jolliffe about the album:

SP: About eight years after working with Froese in Berlin, you wrote to him. What was his response?
SJ: I wrote to Edgar in the late-1970s congratulating him on the release of *Rubycon*. I felt it was a milestone in electronic music. He called me and asked if I would be interested in re-joining. And so began the birth of *Cyclone*.
SP: Having arrived at Audio Studios in Berlin, how did the *Cyclone*

sessions begin for you? Was there a musical goal in mind – something quite progressive, perhaps?
SJ: Working on *Cyclone* was quite exhausting. I felt I was doing most of the driving. There seemed to be a lot of apathy and a lack of commitment. I would often spend many hours alone in the studio creating ideas. On 'Rising Runner Missed By Endless Sender', I played all of the instruments apart from the drums and a bit of sequencer. I had no preconceived ideas as usual, but just let things appear as naturally as possible. The vocals were just another direction and I wasn't sure we should keep them, but Edgar seemed to feel they were a good move.
SP: Your flute and reeds-playing – flute in particular – on *Cyclone,* has always struck me as being *voice-like*. Do you feel a flute is a kind of voice?
SJ: I have always pushed the limits of the instruments I use. Combining voice for me, helped to express my thoughts.
SP: Could you say a few words about the lyrics to 'Rising Runner Missed By Endless Sender' and 'Bent Cold Sidewalk'?
SJ: I write lyrics in the same manner as music – sort of improvised words, a bit like an open prayer grabbing at the source trying to be a tool for unspoken thoughts. Of course, I scribbled down lots of ideas, but most of it came straight to the page. Other parts I just improvised straight onto tape. After creating them, I am almost a listener reading them back. Some of it makes sense, other parts I am still not sure. It was exactly the same for 'Bent Cold Sidewalk'. Even the titles appeared out of nowhere, including 'Madrigal Meridian'.
SP: What are your memories of making 'Madrigal Meridian'?
SJ: 'Madrigal Meridian' could have been a performance at a gig – we all joined in on a long improvisation. I added a lot of Lyricon afterwards, like violin and trumpet sounds. I imagined I was a gypsy violinist. At the end, I created a lot of different lines on the Lyricon. Unfortunately, a lot of it was lost. I had meant it to be a sort of canon with interweaving lines.
SP: What is a Lyricon and how do you play it?
SJ: The Lyricon was made by a little company in the USA. They wanted to fly me over to demonstrate it, but I declined: yet another plane ride. It was a very impressive instrument made of chromium metal with fingering like a sax. It was wired up to a box that produced some lovely sounds. No saving of sounds or midi in those days, but a very expressive instrument. They were bought out by Yamaha, who produced a version called a WX7 which I still use now. I sold my Lyricon to The Moody Blues.

SP: The inner photo of the *Cyclone* album had the four of you in unusual pose: what was the meaning of that photo pose?
SJ: I have always wondered what that was about. I was doing my usual thing and grabbing the moment. The doll was a sort of mascot that I took along to the gigs and sat her on the piano. It belonged to Monique (Edgar's first wife). Unfortunately, I never saw it again after the tour – apparently, one of the roadies had broken her.
SP: What do you think music is? For you, is it about expression of inner states and feelings (e.g., when playing flute or reeds)?
SJ: Music creation is a way for me to express my feelings as well as the enjoyment of the craft. It has always fascinated me from childhood: both the spiritual connection and the emotional one. There seems to be a source that drives these ideas, and I need to develop a technic to collect and express them.
SP: Do you think technology sometimes masks or impedes the human expression of music?
SJ: Technic is just a means of arriving at a statement. The tools can be anything from a piece of bone to a complicated piece of software. We have to make an honest choice.

Cyclone (1978)

Personnel:
Edgar Froese: Moog, synths, Mellotron, electric guitar, acoustic guitar
Chris Franke: Moog, synths, Mellotron, electronic drums
Steve Jolliffe: vocals, flute, piccolo, cor anglais, bass clarinet, Hohner clavinet, synths, grand piano, Fender Rhodes, tenor horns, soprano horns, Lyricon
Klaus Krieger: polyester custom-built drums with multi-trigger unit, electronic drum, Paiste cymbals, bubims, Burma gong set
Producer: Tangerine Dream
Recorded at Audio Studios, Berlin: January 1978
Release date: UK and US: March 1978
Chart placings: UK: 37
Running time: 38:33
All tracks by Tangerine Dream
Side One: 1. 'Bent Cold Sidewalk' 2. 'Rising Runner Missed By Endless Sender'
Side Two: 1. 'Madrigal Meridian'

Following the departure of Peter Baumann, Froese and Franke were left on their own. That change in personnel however led them to a brave

new direction, which over the coming two years would yield the richest of rewards.

The first harbinger of that new direction was Steve Jolliffe, whom Froese had known since his earliest days in Berlin. A gifted instrumentalist, Jolliffe lent his considerable talents to what would become the first of a glorious pair of progressive electronic LP releases, stretching the band's music far beyond previous strictures. The second harbinger was the arrival of Klaus Krüger (aka Klaus Krieger), a superb drummer whom Froese had known since the early 1960s.

The album opens with 'Bent Cold Sidewalk', and at once we are in new territory as a mysterious vocoder voice intones a chant in electronic style. Then, with a whoosh of synths, the drums come in with bass synths, chords and a melodic theme, before Jolliffe's reedy voice begins singing. The lyrics are surreal and enigmatic – like most of Froese's song titles – though there are hints of human themes (living life 'a long long time' for instance) as Jolliffe doubletracks his way through the vocals. Mellotron brass complements each verse. The melody is memorable and the feel overall progressive; an assured beginning to the new sound.

After this first section, the drums stop and an ambient bridge takes the listener into the next part, which, opening with a sequence, is more familiar territory. Almost at once a flute begins soloing over the sequence and light string synth backing, showing again how confident the band are of their new direction. It is all beautifully played and arranged. New synths counterpoint the flute, then a bass note anchors the sequence before Jolliffe returns playing reeds and a breathy, high-register flute, around which new synths dance. The whole composition is very light, yet perfectly arranged, as each instrument takes a turn with others in support and counterpoint.

After a while the mood becomes darker, as Jolliffe's voice returns, at first breathy, then emotional, even pained, uttering vocalisations whose meanings can only be guessed. The sequences then develop – new synths, more flute, and voices swirling in and around the mix, before Krieger's drums add a pounding rhythm. As the music pulls back, a melodic theme emerges, and the string synths, so well utilised on this album, dive beneath the mix.

As the sequences fade, the first theme returns, announced once again by Krieger's drums and the Mellotron brass. Jolliffe restates his melody. The Mellotron brass is high in the mix here, ushering in a new melodic part for Jolliffe to sing, in which he returns to a more emotional, even anguished vocal style, double-tracked with a harmony in his voice's lower register. At the end of this section, there is more wordless vocalisation, as the Mellotron and synths take the music into the finale, which Krieger ably supports. Though it came out of the blue for fans of the band, this whole section – once the listener has come to terms with the new direction – is a masterclass in composition: melodic, brilliantly arranged, with emotional subtlety and power.

Side A's second vocal track is 'Rising Runner Missed By Endless Sender' – more surreal lyrics, again with drums, synths and sequences in support. The melody is not quite as direct as that which preceded it, but it is still strong, Joliffe singing in both a low and a high register. We have to guess who the 'Rising Runner' is and where he is running, but that is part of the track's vibe: one reason it can be returned to again and again. The lyrics are evocative of environments – howling winds, coloured stones and spaces hard to fold, with the 'Endless Sender' somewhere not too far away. As with the first cut, instrumental bridges link the different sung sections, and the string synth is given prominence. Jolliffe uses a mixture of comprehensible words and weird vocalisations, a terrifically effective style.

Side B is taken up by one of the group's all-time classics, 'Madrigal Meridian' (a track prefigured by 'Nights Of Automatic Women' on Froese's similarly progressive *Ages*). It opens with a particularly mysterious ambient section of woozy synths and subtle, unexpected pitch and key changes. The mood shifts when a rippling sequence oscillating in a fast tempo sounds out, followed by deeper synths, and then a loping, rhythmic loop which, as the music progresses, becomes ever higher in pitch: evocative perhaps of strange industrial landscapes. As the background synths fade and the loop reaches its highest pitch, a new sequence enters, then a melodic theme from the Mellotron brass. Almost at once Krieger's drums begin, and then the track is off on its wonderful journey, a headlong rush of drums, the insistent sequence, and blaring, exotic Mellotron brass, underpinned by various synthesizers. This section powers along with great intensity, evoking some high technology environment of futuristic vehicles.

As the sequences mutate, a new, softer synth enters the mix, with white noise whooshes in the background and some subtle variation in Krieger's cymbal work. A new, double-speed sequence underpins the whole, diving around the mix as the main melodic solo continues. Then another of those woozy pitch/key changes emerges from underneath, before stabilising and returning to the main theme, again played on the Mellotron brass. Krieger's drums pick up new rhythmic alterations, counterpointing the Mellotron, before a new sequence emerges – this time very fast – against which Krieger plays much more freely, taking out the main rhythm to support the new rippling sequence, before returning to the 4/4 time signature. As this new sequence re-emerges, it plays a long-form melody, as if composed from elements of the original sequence, rarely repeating, like an incredibly fast and complex synth solo. Most likely this part was programmed note-by-note into the sequencer.

As wailing synths announce a new section, the basic sequence changes, though the drums never alter (a brilliant bit of mixing here), and the trip continues with Froese playing an extended guitar solo – one of his best studio recordings, in fact, melodic and varied, with Krieger and the new sequence in constant support.

As the breathless Froese fades out, a new sound takes over the solo part: the Lyricon, in 1978 a new instrument, part breath-powered, part keyboard. This beautiful solo sounds like some exotic violin bouncing over the sequences, under which Krieger varies his drum patterns with brilliant precision. As the music ebbs, swells and ebbs again, new string synths enter, followed by a novel variation on the Lyricon. Then the chord sequence alters subtly, telling the listener they are on the trip's concluding part. More Lyricons come in – some deeply reverberated – and then the drums and sequences fade together, as a wash of string synths both support and pull the Lyricon solos down.

As these paired Lyricon solos fade, a chiming, stately harpsichord enters, against which the string synths begin a new chord sequence. Suddenly, the mood is formal; strange after that free-floating, breathless flight. Bass notes and another string synth emerge, taking the music into a fuller sound, before the harpsichord starts a second melodic pattern. Now Jolliffe's flute returns, playing a joyous, airy solo, matching the solemn harpsichord with something much lighter. At the conclusion of this short piece, there is another unexpected change of mood as a backwards-sounding synth intones a five-note riff, before – at the very end – a final Lyricon insert floats free and unaccompanied, like a 'Last Post' bugle call played for the dead of the far future.

With 'Madrigal Meridian', Tangerine Dream proved – if proof were needed – that in a few short years they had progressed way beyond their avant-garde roots and improvisational methods into something of enormous musical confidence, variety and complexity. This side-long cut stands as one of their triumphs, enjoyable even after hundreds of listens.In 1994,

Steve Jolliffe gave an interview to Jeff Filbert, published at *dreamcircle.com*, in which he elaborated on the album's recording:

> It was conceived totally from scratch in a 48-track recording studio that was booked 24 hours a day for a month. We all went in together at first, trying lots of ideas and improvising, but we had some difficulty focusing our musical vision collectively ... I did most of the tracks on it except for the bass and drum parts, which were performed by Chris and Klaus. After that, things seemed to go much smoother and our ideas jelled better.

Mixing proved to be an interesting task:

> We all had a go at the mixing. We used two 24-track recording machines synced together to make the needed 48 tracks. I remember at one point, we all became ill, one after another, being stuck in the studio all the time without proper ventilation. Edgar would be mixing and get sick, and while he was laid up, I'd try mixing. Then I would be laid-up, and Chris would try mixing. This process went on for some time ... There were things going on in all of them, so every time we would mix, it would be like a new album. *Cyclone* was the result of several different mixes, or at least the best part of them. We could have made three albums out of those sessions. I'd love to go back and remix it with some of the tracks that we didn't use. There were flute quartets on some sections and some other things as well: all that was lost.

March saw the release of the album (adorned with a beautiful cover painting by Froese) and a European tour, with dates in Britain, France, Germany, Spain and Belgium. This was a very successful tour with a Laserium light show: many of the dates sold out. One of these concerts – the 24 February date at the Audimax in Hamburg – made it to a formal recording, being released in the blue box *Bootleg Box Set Volume 2*.

In the interview for this book, I asked Steve Jolliffe about the Cyclone Tour:

> SP: What are your memories of the *Cyclone* Tour?
> SJ: Hard work; every sound check was a nightmare. Nobody seemed to know how to set up a microphone, and most nights, I was still shouting at the roadies while the promoters were desperate to open the doors. I have always been comfortable with playing live. I don't suffer from stage

fright and I immerse myself in the moment. It's good to know I was tolerated.

SP: How was it playing with Laserium in attendance?

SJ: Laserium were fascinating and very creative. I will always remember them lighting joints with the laser beam. The world of colour is an obvious marriage for instrumental music. I have since spent a lot of time developing animation to create a similar environment.

SP: What was your personal approach to playing live?

SJ: I always try to capture my current feelings and go with the development that arises from my immediate thoughts. A great privilege to communicate with so many people at once.

SP: Did you enjoy the *Cyclone* Tour?

SJ: On stage was enjoyable, but that's only a small part of touring. It was exhausting and I was pleased to take a break.

This tour made a strong impression on those who saw it. Steve Dinsdale of electronic music titans Radio Massacre International remembers it vividly:

Some gigs are hazy; this one is still very real in the memory. Newcastle City Hall 23rd March 1978. I was the oldest at 15; the youngest in our party was 12. The dry ice, the lasers, and there they were almost close enough to touch; Edgar in clear view in denim waistcoat, Steve emitting otherworldly and frightening sounds, Klaus powering away alongside Chris' Moog sequences. We could scarcely believe we were there; it was almost too real. And with the open minds of the young, we fully accepted it all. Over the last year, we'd heard the mighty *Encore*; investigated *Alpha Centauri* and *Atem, Ages, Rubycon, Sorcerer* ... we were ready for anything, and we got Tangerine Dream, the space-rock band. Denim-clad hordes with embroidered Rush logos and *Tarkus* covers ... the aroma (and maybe even the effect) of what we would later come to know as hash, filling the air, and yes, a couple of rows in front of us, a seated headbanger: hair flying relentlessly in all directions. A medal of endurance for that man!

Electronic music afficionado and British EM promoter Dave Buxton also recalled that magical tour of 1978:

I had paid my £3:00 and had a precious ticket to attend. I was seventeen and not used to going to concerts, and especially not those outside

> Nottingham at the time, so I eagerly clambered into the back of my friend's car, wondering if the beaten up old thing could get us there. You are never worried about getting back when you go to a gig ... I remember being impressed by how big the venue was compared with others I had been in, and was pleasantly surprised to be a really good vantage point in the middle of the stalls. It was the *Cyclone* tour, and it's a pity no recordings seem to have survived of that night, because the concert was awesome from start to finish. Steve Jolliffe was all energy, and strutted around the stage like a kind of electronic Ian Anderson or pixie from Planet Gong. Klaus Kruger's drums were wonderful, adding another visual and auditory side to the performance. Froese and Franke were pretty static throughout, behind their keyboards and machines, but generating and driving the music forward. The sound was clear as a bell, and it was certain they were on form. The audience was in the mood as well. It was a real symbiotic kind of atmosphere, with each feeding off the other. They played the album but used the long track as a jumping-off spot to go into a long improvised piece. In some of the recordings I've heard, this didn't exactly work too well, but this night I was spellbound by the driving sequences, flute and drums. I remember the two vocal tracks working really well also ... One thing will never fade, and that is the amazing visual experience that Laserium provided. Kruger's drums were rigged into floor lights which sent coloured beams of lights from the floor upwards as he played. While this was going on, lasers played on the ceiling and walls: constantly morphing away. Many other lights seemed to bathe the stage as well, making it a totally visual explosion of colour and awe as the band played. It was one of those gigs that seemed to flash by ... This was a different Tangerine Dream from the time I had seen them before. Vocals, visual and full of energy. It rocked. The trip back to Nottingham seemed to last five minutes as the adrenaline continued to flow in the four attendees who had been at a special event. This has always remained my favourite Tangerine Dream concert I ever attended; with *Cyclone* one of my favourite albums.

Critics were less kind about the album itself. In an interview given to *Melody Maker* in October 1994, Froese discussed his thoughts:

> I understood the criticism at that time, but it wasn't anything new to us. As far back as I can recall, some people have thought we're geniuses and

> others have dismissed as a bunch of dumb knob twiddlers. So what? I think it's fair to respect all opinions.

By summer, however, Jolliffe went on his way, leaving Froese and Franke to record with Krieger what would become a defining moment of electronic progressive rock.

1979 – Progression, Music, Digital

One of the signs of a great group is how they react to change. With Jolliffe departing following the *Cyclone* Tour, the trio of Froese, Franke and Krieger decided to decamp to Hansa Studios in Berlin in August and September 1978 to work on new music. And what extraordinary music it was. Released in February 1979, *Force Majeure* – presented on transparent vinyl with a gorgeous front cover painting by Monique Froese – was a suite of quite exceptional quality.

Force Majeure (1979)

Personnel:
Edgar Froese: synths, electric guitar, acoustic guitar
Chris Franke: Moog synth and sequencer, synths
Klaus Krieger: drums and percussion
Eduard Meyer: cello
Producer: Tangerine Dream and Eduard Meyer
Recorded at Hansa Studios, Berlin: August-September 1978
Release date: UK and US: February 1979
Chart placings: UK: 37
Running time: 40:14
All tracks by Tangerine Dream
Side One: 1. 'Force Majeure'
Side Two: 1. 'Cloudburst Flight' 2. 'Thru Metamorphic Rocks'

Though *Cyclone* was a marvellous album of great originality, the best of Tangerine Dream's two-year foray into progressive styles was yet to come. *Force Majeure,* their final album of the 1970s, would sum up everything they were and had achieved – their burgeoning musicality, their ability with complex arrangements and mixes, their playing, and their overall vision of a music unfettered by cliche. Like its predecessor, the album would have a side-long epic on one side and two tracks on the other. But this time, though Klaus Krieger remained, Jolliffe was not present, and the music returned to purely instrumental vistas. Yet while *Cyclone* was an album about surreal environments and situations, *Force Majeure* was an album of journeys *between* environments: of the act of travelling. Its ethos was of excursions across the face of the globe and even – at the end – beneath it.

Opening with a spine-tingling phased effects introduction, a synth sounding like a vocal chant soon takes up a gothic theme as the phasing and effects mutate and transmute underneath. Over this a fragment of synth birdsong echoes, until – after a couple of minutes – the mood changes into something more stable and encouraging: dense chords, whizzing white noise, a tinkling melodic theme, and then the beauty of Eduard Meyer's keening cello. Now string synths come to the fore, supporting the cello. After a key change, this cello returns, ever more hopeful in mood: dawn after night perhaps.

As the introduction fades, a simple synth intones a few notes, before piano and keyboards declare the first melodic theme and its associated chord sequence. Then Krieger's drums come in alongside Froese's electric guitar, and the journey is underway. Like its predecessor 'Madrigal Meridian', this track has enormous forward momentum, phrased in elegant guitar chopping (the melodic theme) and in Krieger's subtle drum work; his cymbal variations are brilliant here. Once the first statement is over, there is a short bridge before the second variation, with an amended chord sequence taking the key down, then up again. Now twin guitars take the listener along, with more fantastic cymbal work from Krieger, who is particularly good on this section.

The second part opens with arpeggiated acoustic guitar and pounding drums, before an eight-note sequence begins, and then the second main theme, this time played on a synthesizer. Again, the sense of forward motion is strong, propelled by the combination of sequences and drums. As more phased string synths take up the theme, the rhythm takes a new, slower tempo, before reverting to the old one, with new synths taking the melodic lead. Each time Krieger and the bridge end a section, a new one builds up, varying, changing, continuing, until the music halts and a vague, enigmatic vocoder sounds out. Then more birdsong effects and a steam train appear, brilliantly plugged into the mix as a travelogue bridge. This steam train is a perfect example of how the band used the smallest, slightest thing to evoke the feelings they wanted in their music; in this case, travel across the planet. The steam train lasts only a few seconds, yet somehow it epitomises the entire track.

But now we are somewhere truly exotic. Effects-laden, high-register voices intone a wordless, keyless music, as if falling from the skies once the train has moved on, accompanied by light synth effects and phased keyboards. But soon, they are gone. Deeper, more swamp-like sounds emerge, then the dense tone of a bass synth, accompanied by a string synth and another effortless guitar solo. This is a bridge theme, however, leading to one of the band's most beloved sequenced sections, introduced by a single real-world bell.

Created from numerous fluttering sequences, this new section seems to float above the land. Melodically and harmonically sophisticated, it surges this way and that, sometimes on changing bass notes, sometimes constant, sometimes set against a light string synth. After a while, the string synth is revealed to be following a melody, which rises and falls as the piece progresses and new synths take up the lead. At length a full melody comes into play, supported by a new chord sequence and a new variation on the fluttering sequences. The music is not only brilliantly composed, it is beautifully arranged: a highlight of the band's studio career.

At the end, however, a new section begins, created from drums and chiming synths, this time with a much earthier mood than the previous vibe of flight and floating. The listener returns to forward motion, and at speed: this music never rests because there are always new lands to discover. As the new melody emerges with its accompanying sequence, we seem to be somewhere half oriental, half occidental – a land of fusion.

Then we are done: destination reached. The synth washes and gothic chords of the introduction return for a brief restatement, then the music fades. It is a pinnacle of the band's studio career.

Side B opens with another piece beloved of fans, 'Cloudburst Flight'. Beginning with twelve-string guitar chords and a backdrop of lush synthesizers, the mood is extraordinarily light, evoking clouds, air, and flying. Froese's elegant chords and single-note inserts describe some gossamer vehicle in which the listener sits, gazing at the fluffy white clouds around them. After this opening, a simple sequence begins, and with it a chord sequence and a new melodic theme: a really lovely one, again emphasising lightness and buoyancy. Then Krieger's cymbals enter the mix, augmenting each part of the music, building up this theme of motion through the clouds. A second melody takes a new direction, albeit with the same structure, but then as the full drums come in a third theme sets the trip underway, a fantastic synth solo flying over it. Partway through, Froese's electric guitar takes on lead duties, elegant, melodic and subtle as before, with his trademark vibrato style and distortion setup. The second part of this solo amplifies the mood, adding emotional intensity, but this part – judging by the change in vibrato and the sound of the solo – was performed to a slowed-down backing tape, making Froese appear to play faster, though in actuality he would have been playing at his usual speed to slower music. It is still a great solo, however, and works in the context of the piece. The drums are also terrific here. Kreiger was a masterful drummer, knowing exactly when to let rip and when to pull back.

After the solo, the music dramatically subsides, paving the way for a gorgeous flute-like synth solo played over a descending chord sequence. As the initial sequence is restated, the music fades as the flight ends.

The second cut on side B, 'Thru Metamorphic Rocks', is a gothic, futuristic, high-tech journey through underground realms. Perhaps more of a traditional piece – it relies mainly on insistent jagged sequences for its effect – the music opens on a piano riff with string synth accompaniment, before weird effects and a harmonic piano variant usher in the drums (again, brilliantly played and arranged) and a new set of gothic synths. Once this part is done, a guitar riff opens a new audio window with its associated set of chords. In this section the listener seems to be looking out of a train window at a dark, earthy landscape rushing by at great speed.

But soon, new effects transmute the music, as the listener enters a junction of sorts: an interchange. As the music fades into high-register distortion and phased effects, a dark, oscillating, tense sequence begins, with a single repeated chord that speaks of a completely new realm – underground, perhaps lit by flickering neon tubes, but profoundly different from the surface environments the previous two tracks described. Heavily-effected drums and crashing cymbals add to the atmosphere of macabre tension. This piece, with its Doppler-shifted synth effects evoking speed, is perhaps the band's greatest music describing travel. You only have to close your eyes with it playing to imagine journeying through underground realms of the far future. It is extraordinarily evocative, especially when the backing synths begin to swell, and then, later on, when strange creatures laugh, howl and cry, as if from the bowels of the earth where only monsters live.

But the journey ends, as all journeys must, even if the listener's final stop is infernal. As whirring chords, eerie voices and backwards effects scurry across the mix, the drums fade, the chord dies away, and all that is left is another howling beast and a melange of synth effects, percussion and a lonely keyboard chord. The engine has powered down. Motion has ceased. We are at the end of the trip. All we can hear now is a vocal pad, indicating terminus.

This last Tangerine Dream album of the 1970s evokes as no other in the band's repertoire the sensation of *motion* – of travel, of air and flight, of rushing underground, of speeding through a variety of exotic lands on the surface of the planet. It is one of their greatest achievements, and of their 1970s albums stands alongside *Rubycon* at the very top of the list.

The album contains one of the most famous Tangerine Dream items of lore, concerning a certain mixing accident. Froese explained the situation in his November 1997 interview with *Soundscapes*:

> 'Thru Metamorphic Rocks' had an accident in the mixing desk. So while we did the recording, the tape ran and all the instruments were locked in, and we played, and we improvised quite a lot all the time. Then all of a sudden, something went wrong with the desk. So there were a lot of strange noises all of a sudden, which appear within the track and are totally wrong, but which actually made sense in the music. We listened to it again and again and said, 'Should we? Shouldn't we?'. Finally, we said, 'Okay, leave it the way it is'.

There were no live dates at all this year, despite the commercial and considerable critical success of *Force Majeure* – their fourth highest-selling LP – which spent seven weeks on the British album chart. Gigs were scheduled, but later cancelled because of relatively poor LP sales in Germany. Froese recalled the happy vibe at Hansa Studios in his 1980 *Neumusik* interview: 'We did it in a seven-week recording session in a good studio in the middle of summer. It was a good feeling, a good atmosphere and nothing to fight about'.

In the group's April 1986 interview with Johnny Black of *thisBEAT*, Franke also recalled that time:

> There's one piece – 'Cloudburst Flight' – which I still enjoy playing. Sometimes, doing something again and again, it loses its power, but this still means a lot to me. It's hard to say what you try to achieve when you make music. Different words come to mind like ... room, landscape, painting, a combination of all the things that make up life.

However, to David Elliott in *Neumusik* fanzine, Froese expanded on the thinking of the time, beginning with his thoughts on the reason for the lack of a tour:

> Yes, there was a reason. We were on the border of overturning everything. We got a 100,000DM laser show, 100,000DM stage equipment. We got everything, and it was so, so superficial ... Anyway, we were going

> to tour after the release of *Force Majeure*. Everything was booked – Wembley in London ... Everything was finalised, but then we decided that the whole thing was just blown up too much. We remembered how we'd started – in the small places.

Elliott asked Froese if he thought groups realised that they were too big:

> That's right. We think it's definitely better to play five times at the Hammersmith (Odeon) than just once at Wembley ... I mean, a lot of bands just play their tape recorders: 50% of the music comes out of their instruments, and the rest is tapes. If you reach that sort of unreal level, or if you're just into the business for doing that sort of thing, then I believe you can't call yourself a musician anymore. You're just a salesman. So we cancelled everything and we decided that we'd go on the road when we were small enough. I think all this big money, kills; the really big tour, kills.

In summer, Froese was in Berlin again, recording the music for his solo album *Stuntman,* which was released in September. But now the group were looking at brand new territory: digital. The end of the 1970s was at hand, and a whole new technological terrain was about to open up, characterizing the sound of the 1980s. How Tangerine Dream adapted to and utilised that terrain showed their continuing brilliance, leading to further success, both critical and commercial. Despite the change from analogue to digital, they would continue to evolve.

For Tangerine Dream, the 1970s were a period of remarkable discovery and progression. By chance, propelled by the vision and energy of Froese and a cohort of friends and helpers, they managed to develop and change creatively, and find commercial success: a rare achievement in the music business. No artists remain entirely free of their commercial success, but some – Kate Bush comes to mind – manage to walk that most difficult of tightropes, balancing creative progression, personal satisfaction and commercial success. Tangerine Dream may not have hit the heights of the album charts, but they sold hundreds of thousands of LPs just in Britain: a notable achievement. Their impact on the musical world of the 1970s was enormous. Ask any electronic musician who their influences are, and Tangerine Dream are likely to be in there. Even some latter-day pop acts count the group as an influence. Kraftwerk were not the *only* electronic band in town.

Tangerine Dream's development through the 1970s in some ways mimics the development of synthesizers, though in various interviews, Froese and Franke insisted that the tools of their trade could have been anything; it so happened that keyboards and synthesizers – developing at great speed at the time – were those tools. The lineup of three synthesizer-playing musicians was groundbreaking. Add to that a lengthy catalogue of improvised concerts, and you have the recipe for one of the most remarkable musical journeys of modern rock.

In due course, however, the decade ended. What lay ahead for the group proved to be very different from what had been undertaken during the 1970s.

Afterwards – Digital, Albums, Berlin

Something shifted in 1980. It could be heard on the first Tangerine Dream album of the new decade, though perhaps its clearest exposition was on Klaus Schulze's *Dig It*. The world of synthesizers, for so long rooted in analogue manufacture – voltage-controlled oscillators and everything related to them – was starting to be replaced by digital machines.

Froese and his group had for some time reaped the benefit of working with new synthesizers, and even some on the cusp of innovation. Only six years had passed since their groundbreaking use of the Moog Modular system to create sequences, yet already they were into the new breed of digital synthesizer, and it showed on their first release of the decade. *Tangram* was a beautiful pair of compositions made by Froese, Franke and new man Johannes Schmoelling, who added keyboard chops to the established duo. But Klaus Krieger's drums, and other acoustic instruments, were out. *Tangram* was primarily digital, using drum machines and a host of synths to mesmerising effect. The album was recorded at Franke's brand new Polygon Studios in Berlin, where Schmoelling in particular contributed to the music's melodic and compositional style.

In a 1994 *Tangents* interview for Mark Prendergast, Schmoelling elaborated:

> Before I joined, I felt the music of Tangerine Dream was basically built on sequencer loops, more or less in one key, with little harmonic changes and long ongoing sessions of improvisation. When I joined, we tried a mixture of more structured elements, with more jazz-orientated chords, composed melodies and synthesizer solos close to rock.

The group's live work changed as a consequence of the new approach. To the disappointment of some fans, the 1980s gigs were based around recapitulations of album pieces, with some improvised work in between, and live solos. The Moog Modular remained, but its use was subtly changed. I saw the group a few times in the early-1980s, the impression of those concerts still vivid in my mind. I and the audiences were wowed by those futuristic digital sounds, with the 1982 concerts particularly noteworthy, not least the one made into the *Logos Live* album.

In his interview published in *Neumusik* fanzine, Franke described the changes in his use of synthesizers around this time. Asked whether or not he still liked the typical sequencer sound as on *Rubycon* side two, for example, he explained the changes in his outlook. Why did he substitute this sound for drum-style rhythms that were more harsh?:

> I used this sequencer for about three or four years – this type of style in various ways – and now I'm going to change from the drum or harsh-type rhythm, to explore transitions between a very soft, new type of medium-sequenced material to a very hard material. I have the dynamics now to make any kind of sound I want, and in my spectrum of interest, there's a definite place for hard sounds, because I like contrasts. If you don't feel the hard sounds, you can't feel the soft sounds as much as you want to.

Froese, meanwhile, explained to David Elliott in *Neumusik*, how he saw the future. Would there be any new directions? Or would it be just a natural progression?:

> Yes, there'll definitely be all of these, but you can't really say what for sure. There should be some sort of new direction. I don't want to call it anything. It's just a feeling.

Their studio work continued to be trailblazing. In 1981 the group released one of its most extraordinary works – the album *Exit* – based around the sounds of the new PPG Wave 2.2 synthesizer and the Fairlight CMI computer. At the time, nothing like the Fairlight had been heard, though soon it would be – Michael Jackson, for example, used the synth/sampler for the opening of 'Beat It' in 1982. The *Exit* album proved once again that Froese and his cohort could produce wonderful music while remaining at the forefront of technological innovation. With Monique Froese's eye-catching cover design, *Exit* was another notable release.

The opening cut 'Kiew Mission' features a Russian actress reciting a monologue about world peace and international communication. Froese strongly supported the anti-nuclear cause, and even had many copies of *Exit* shipped and distributed to – as he put it – 'Different people in Russia, people in the political power structure, in the arts, and just to the ordinary Russian people too'. In the album's press release, Froese explained why he did all this:

> The words are directed at people in Russia. It's a very spiritual message we hope will ease the situation over here. If you're in Europe right

> now, you would see that all people talk about the Third World War. As musicians, we can use our music to say something about the positive side, and hope our message gets through.

1982 saw the release of *White Eagle* – another gorgeous digital symphony, with a side-long epic and three shorter pieces, including the title track, which showed the group could use melody to marvellous effect. Overall, the album was another step into the digital world, now being enthusiastically taken up by many electronic musicians. Schulze in this year released his final work of genius, the remarkable double LP *Audentity*.

Film work continued to pour in – the group now recognised in the field for their talent and approach – and the soundtrack to the film *Thief* was released in 1981, reusing to slightly peculiar effect a section from 'Thru Metamorphic Rocks'. Other soundtracks were recorded, with some not released until much later. Only in 2020 – in the retrospective box set *Pilots Of Purple Twilight* – did two previously unreleased soundtracks see the light of day, *The Soldier* (1982, directed by James Glickenhaus) and 1983's *The Keep,* directed by Michael Mann (the latter a famous *unknown* for Tangerine Dream fans).

The other notable release was the live album *Logos Live*, from the group's 6 November 1982 concert at the Dominion Theatre, London, which I attended. Fifty minutes of music was extracted from the two-hour recording, with the full concert seeing the light of day 38 years later on *Pilots Of Purple Twilight.* The concert was stunning, especially some of the digital voice sections – one part had a chant of 'Edgar!' running through it – although a debt to the work of Steve Reich was obvious. The event was also visually stunning, with excellent use of lights and backdrop.

1983 saw other soundtracks and another studio album. *Hyperborea* was the last album Virgin Records released over the decade span of the contract (renegotiated in 1978). The album saw a further development in the group's digital and melodic style, but some of the music sounded a little limp in comparison with *White Eagle* and *Exit,* though the three shorter tracks were all superb.

In Mark Prendergast's 1994 interview for the *Tangents* box set, Schmoelling recalled the time:

> Like *Logos Live, Hyperborea* was determined by the new generation of digital synthesizers and sampling technology. We were able to memorise

sounds, and used a lot of sampled drum sounds. We invented new rhythm structures by using a special arpeggiator technique, and so on. The title 'No Man's Land' was influenced by the film *Gandhi* and its brilliant soundtrack.

The first new soundtrack was for the film *Risky Business,* with Tangerine Dream's contribution being mostly previously released tracks, edited and retitled to correspond to film scenes. A second soundtrack was for Mike Gray's film *Wavelength,* with the music again edited from earlier recordings, including pieces from *Quichotte* (1981), *Tangram*, *Exit*, and a cut from Froese's solo album *Kamikaze 1989*.

Quichotte, though, was a significant release, being edited down from two live concerts played on 31 January 1980 at the Palast der Republik, East Berlin (Schmoelling's public debut). The title was a reference to a film version of *Don Quixote* being shown at a cinema not far away. Released in 1986 as *Pergamon* – though it had received a minimal release on the East German Amiga label in 1980 – this album again showed the group in imperious live form, with Froese's guitar solo on 'Quichotte Part II' being of particular interest. It should be noted, however, that sections of this second part were put together in the studio, and when Tangerine Tree 17 emerged – recorded from the radio broadcast – the differences between *Quichotte* and the live gig were obvious.

Well-known music journalist Jonathan Miller interviewed Froese about this concert:

The Palast der Republik was where parliament sessions were held and important political speeches made, so we had to agree not to make any political statements and just play music; nothing that would collide with the political system. Since it was the first concert of a Western band in East Berlin, and in such a high-profile place, all the international press were outside, with cameras everywhere, because 80% of the tickets were given away to officials and organisations connected with the East German government. The remaining 20% sold out in about five minutes. About half an hour prior to the show, there was a very delicate moment because 900 people were pressing against the venue's huge glass windows trying to get in. Inside, we had to make a decision: Did we want lots of publicity by allowing the windows to be damaged – maybe people would be hurt or worse – and blowing the gig? A public relations company would say we were stupid, but from my perspective of performing our music, it

> was very simple – I told the officials we would not perform unless they let those people in for free, thus preventing any trouble. They did, and that was the first time I found out exactly what political journalism was all about: Writing something sensational and extraordinary brings success, but at what expense? On the other hand, we had a wonderful concert. As far as the music was concerned, it was just great; but for political international journalism, it was a total disappointment. The entire gig just got one small mention in a daily newspaper the next day: no one was really interested. If we were to do it again today, I would make exactly the same decision.

Still the soundtrack work kept coming: *Firestarter* and *Flashpoint,* both soundtracks composed by the trio of Froese, Franke and Schmoelling.

Of more note, perhaps, was the 1983 live album *Poland* (released in November 1984). Recorded on 10 December at the Torwar Hall, Warsaw, during a taboo-busting visit to the communist country – then only four months on from the communist government's period of martial law – the album documented a superb concert in which the group used Roland, Yamaha and PPG Wave 2.2 synthesizers to great effect. Especially beautiful was the opening few minutes of the Side A title track, which showed the group's compositional skill in all its glory. The album was the first to be released away from Virgin Records, Jive Electro being the label.

Froese commented on the European political situation and the group's relation to it in his April 1986 interview with Johnny Black of *thisBeat*:

> We've been called a political band, but when we played East Germany and Poland, it was not for political reasons. We just wanted to play to the people there ... After all, what is politics in our time? You might call it crime, Mafia, whatever, instead of politics. Everybody knows that. And not just in some countries, but all of them.

Through these years Froese had continued to make full use of his solo catalogue at Virgin, with new 1980s releases being *Kamikaze 1989* (a film soundtrack), and *Pinnacles*, which sounds much like the digital music the group were pioneering at the time. Like *Epsilon In Malaysian Pale*, this latter album was named for a feature of the Australian landscape – this time the Pinnacles, limestone formations in Nambung National Park, close by the town Cervantes in Western Australia, which Froese was particularly fond of. However, no more solo studio albums would appear for over twenty years.

In 1985, a second Jive Electro release was the next Tangerine Dream studio album after *Hyperborea*, and it turned out to be a particularly significant one. Called *Le Parc*, its concept was based on various parks set in global locations: Bois de Boulogne in Paris, New York's Central Park, Gaudi Park in Guell Garden Barcelona, Berlin's Tiergarten, the Zen Garden at the Ryoanji Temple in Kyoto, Le Parc itself (L.A. – Streethawk), Hyde Park in London, the Cliffs in Sydney, and Yellowstone Park in the Rocky Mountains, America. Not only significant for the excellence of its music, the album also turned out to be the last one in which Johannes Schmoelling played a part: he departed the group in October. But the album showed that Tangerine Dream's flame still burned bright. The compositions were uniformly excellent, the feel vibrant, and Monique Froese's cover design matched the album perfectly. Another significant addition was one of the guest artists, Clare Torry, who sang the evocative and thrilling vocal on the final track. Perhaps listeners should not have been too surprised, given that Froese was much influenced by Pink Floyd in his early days – Torry sang the extraordinary improvised vocal on the *Dark Side Of The Moon* track 'The Great Gig In The Sky'.

Music journalist Jonathan Miller asked Froese to comment on *Le Parc*:

> Tangerine Dream is like breathing – the first twelve or thirteen years was breathing out, and the other decade is breathing in. The simple concept is the inside and outside world. It's more complicated if you go into it, but breathing in means that by the natural aspect of breathing, it's inside and not spacey. It's not macrocosm, it's microcosm.

In 1986 a curious hybrid release appeared: *Green Desert* (see Chapter 5). The album was based on recordings made in summer of 1973 when Peter Baumann briefly departed the band to travel in Nepal and India. At this point the group was between record labels, having departed Ohr but not yet come into contact with Richard Branson. The music Froese and Franke made for the *Green Desert* sessions was intended to act as a taster for what Tangerine Dream could do. But with the advent of Virgin Records and the Manor Studio, the project was shelved, unfinished, leading to *Phaedra*... until 1984, when Froese rediscovered the tapes. However, the sounds on the released album in 1986 suggested that extra, more modern keyboards had been used to add new sounds to the originally recorded music. *Green Desert* is by no means a poor album, but the way it was put together turned out to be a grim precursor to events which followed.

With Schmoelling departed, Froese invited a musician called Paul Haslinger to join the group, which he did for five years. The first studio album to feature Haslinger was *Underwater Sunlight,* offering a varied and interesting selection of music. Haslinger – a jazz and funk musician spotted in a Vienna club – was not used to the group's style and was considerably younger than the two veterans, but the trio worked well together and he stayed.

Studio releases followed at the rate of roughly one per year: *Tyger* (featuring vocals), *Optical Race*, *Lily On The Beach*, *Melrose* and more...

What happened to the group's music in that latter half of the 1980s? I can only give my personal opinion, which I support by noting that exactly the same thing happened to Klaus Schulze at exactly the same time. In the days of Ohr and through the great majority of the Virgin years, the musicians in Tangerine Dream had to struggle to manage and use the synthesizers at their disposal. In some cases, they had to fight. Equipment problems were common in the early days. In addition, the group were using equipment of considerable novelty, in some cases for the first time on record – the Moog Modular system, for instance, used by Franke to create sequences in 1974, or the Wave PPG 2.2 synth. This struggle gave the group their edge. They could take nothing for granted. They had to *work.* They had to make an *effort.* They had to struggle against technical and logistical problems if they were to make the music they had in mind. But this was not only the case with synthesizers. Froese observed that Tangerine Dream's music could have gone down some non-synthesizer route, in which case it would still have been on the edge of musical taste and normality. But as the music on the four Ohr LPs showed, they would still have had to work and make an effort. That music was never going to be *easy.*

By the time we get to the mid-1980s, however, digital synthesizers could do most if not all of the musicians' work. Too many Tangerine Dream albums – and indeed those of many an electronic artist – consisted of short, bland pieces dominated by preset sounds. There was no need to struggle anymore – no technical issues, or studios dominated by multitrack recorders. Then came the advent of hard-disk recording with computers, outboard effects, and much more. It all added up to a relatively easier walk.

In my opinion it is this technological fact that, year by year, in a process of incremental musical debilitation, led to the loss of Tangerine Dream's musical drive. Making music became *easy.* Too easy. There was no need to struggle, so they didn't bother. The albums lost their spark, their originality, their bite, their *surprise* – except in that it was a surprise to hear such bland music from a band formerly so innovative. But almost nobody innovates when synth manufacturers do all that for you.

For Klaus Schulze – creator of some of the most exceptional electronic music LPs from 1975 to 1982, almost all of which were stunning or groundbreaking in some way – the same thing happened. After *Audentity*, *Angst*, and the pretty good (but not amazing) LP *Inter*Face*, he drifted off into a series of non-essential albums of questionable significance, only to re-emerge in 2005 with *Moonlake*, and in 2007 with *Kontinuum*: both returns to form. The same thing happened to Schulze protegee Robert Schröder, albeit half a decade later following his album *Hamaja.* His *Harmonic Ascent, Floating Music, Galaxie Cygnus-A, Paradise* and *Brain Voyager* were all wonderful, with the former releases created through thick and thin during failed attempts to interest labels in electronic music.

Art can be easy when it's inspired, and inspiration comes from many sources, not just struggle. But nothing worth doing is easy. Perhaps for Tangerine Dream pressing a button became the replacement for struggling with a VCO or fighting a reel-to-reel machine.

For many Tangerine Dream fans, though, the music continued to be relevant and worth buying, and through the 1990s and beyond a further slew of studio releases arrived – *Rockoon, Quinoa, Turn Of The Tides, Tyranny Of Beauty, Ambient Monkeys, Mars Polaris, Purgatorio* and *Jeanne d'Arc* in 2005. That year also saw the release of *Phaedra 2005*, in which Froese (now on his own Eastgate label) decided for some reason to re-record *Phaedra*: an album seen by almost his entire fan base – not to mention a great many music historians – as a career-defining classic. But in 2005, aged 61, he was a very different man to the youthful, driven nonentity of the late-1960s Berlin underground. He had lived a musical life. He had made a deep impression upon the world. He had seen the good side of the music industry and tasted every one of its many dark sides. But perhaps the notion of setting up the Eastgate Records label at that time suggested to him a new beginning; a new way to control his musical output, and therefore his career. Whatever the motivation, the album itself was a dreadful mishmash of ambient noodling, which almost no Tangerine Dream fan admits to liking. Most fans rate this album a 1. In fact, it deserves a 0.

However, 2005 also saw a more interesting release from the back catalogue, albeit one shelved because of intra-group tensions at the time of creation. *Kyoto* was recorded in 1983 when the group toured Japan for the first time. Froese and Schmoelling wrote and recorded various pieces of music intended to be performed during the tour and released later as an LP. The tour was a success, but due to tensions within the group the music was shelved in a dark cupboard somewhere. Much later, Froese and Schmoelling decided to release *Kyoto* as a CD, restoring the original tapes for that purpose. The album is very good, showcasing the synths of the time, and the group's compositional and arranging skills, which, in 1983, were still of a very high standard.

2007 saw an album which gave an explicit nod to Froese's hero Syd Barrett of Pink Floyd. *Madcap's Flaming Duty* was an album featuring that rarest of Tangerine Dream events: vocals. A tribute to Barrett, who died in 2006, the album's title was a reference to his solo work *The Madcap Laughs. Madcap's Flaming Duty* was the first album to include new member Bernhard Beibl on guitars, a musician who would remain with the group until 2014.

Other new members arrived around this time – notably Thorsten Quaeschning, whom Froese invited to join in 2005, though Quaeschning had played live in various contexts for a couple of years before that. The saxophonist Linda Spa was a member for many years, as was Froese's son Jerome, who stayed with the group for many years following his guest debut on *Lily On The Beach* in 1989. Other members included synthesist Ulrich Schnauss, violinist Hoshiko Yamane, percussionist Iris Camaa and guitarist Zlatko Perica.

Tours and live albums also continued worldwide. Those albums included *Livemiles* and *Tournado.* Of considerable interest to the fans though were bootleg recordings, especially those dating from the 1970s. In 2002, a fan-run project called Tangerine Tree began the assembly of all the best recordings known to exist of such bootlegged concerts, leading to a remarkable collection of music. The year after, some of those live concerts appeared on Sanctuary Records' seven-disc CD compilation *Bootleg Box Set Volume 1*: the so-called 'orange box'. This collection featured classic concerts: Sheffield 1974; Royal Albert Hall parts one, two and three from 1975; Croydon 1975, parts one, two and three; Bilbao parts one, two, three and four, and Electronic Rock At The Philharmonics, i.e., Berlin 1976. A second box set – the 'blue box' – was released the following year and featured more classic concerts: Nottingham 1976, Washington Lisner Auditorium from 1977, Hamburg Audimax 1978, Newcastle in 1981, and Frankfurt Fassbinder memorial concert of 11 June

1983. These two box sets showed the group's depth and range over its most inspirational decade. Other remastered classic concerts followed.

Tangerine Tree continued, moving from strength to strength over four years. Originating in an attempt to rescue ancient cassette tapes and transfer them to the digital realm, the project was started by collector Heiko Heerssen: the man whom the group granted permission to undertake the work, assisted by mastering engineer Wouter Bessels. This Heerssen instituted in January 2002, asking fans at the online Tangerine Dream discussion group to gather all the tapes they knew of. This formal request generated a considerable number of unknown recordings and other delights, all of which were included. Over the 1970s, the group had been recorded by many fans in their audiences, and these tapes had been traded and passed around for years. Such tapes, however, fixed in ferric oxide, were susceptible to decay. There was therefore a time limit to their lives.

The goal of Tangerine Tree was to preserve and distribute all of the group's known bootleg recordings, focusing on unreleased live concerts but with some additional material. It all had to be done on a strictly non-commercial basis. In the end, almost three hundred hours of recordings were assembled. Many of these were audience recordings (I myself owned a second-generation cassette copy of the 6 May 1976 Manchester gig, sent to me by the man who recorded the concert), but other sources included soundboard recordings, some recordings from FM radio and television broadcasts, and in a few cases the purchase of actual studio master tapes. Consideration was given to recording quality in particular. (A spin-off project called Tangerine Leaves collected recordings deemed not quite fit for the main project.) The project was discontinued in October 2006, but since then all the recordings have made it to the internet, mostly via YouTube.

As the 2010s progressed, Froese continued to record and play live, with – in some cases – the line between group and solo work becoming somewhat blurred. For instance, the pair of albums *Summer In Nagasaki* and *Winter In Hiroshima*, were released under the group name, but really were solo works. A couple of Tangerine Dream box sets also contained solo music.

In his interview given for this book, Steve Schroyder described a significant and emotional event with his friend Froese:

In 1985 or 1986, I was visiting Edgar in Berlin, and I had some money and wanted to buy some instruments. Edgar said, 'Well, you don't need to

> look out for a keyboard – I'm giving you my Memorymoog'. Wow! That's great. So I got his Memorymoog. I don't know why ... perhaps because we made some nice music together. When I met Jerome two years ago (2019), he told me there were three things concerning synthesizers that Edgar regretted: giving me the Memorymoog, giving the PPG synthesizer, and one other. Jerome said he regretted those instrument losses because he loved them. But, it is too bad! The Memorymoog is down in my studio and I still like to play it very much; it's a great instrument. And I love Edgar because it was easy to be with him; we could be like children together somehow, open and honest, nothing behind. I always loved him in my life together with him.

But in these years the end was nearer than Froese could know. In 2014 he slipped on ice while out walking his dog, breaking his jaw, and this accident seems to have had a significant impact on his health. Yet even a few years before this incident some commentators noticed that Froese seemed to be in poor physical shape. No particular conclusions were drawn at the time, at least not in public. On 20 January 2015, however, Froese died of a pulmonary embolism, his son Jerome announcing his death.

Some artists, as they reach the ends of their lives, are reluctant to summarise that life, either in music or in words: Neil Young being a notable example. Many musicians believe such a deed might be a jinx. Froese had just finished writing his autobiography – *Tangerine Dream Force Majeure*: a 380-page hardback tome with 48 pages of photographs – on which he had been working for seven years. Written in a style matching his surreal musical mode, the book recalled many of his life events and many of the people he met, and his fans received it enthusiastically. Whether the autobiography's eventual publication had any psychological effect on its author can never be known, but it is a strange coincidence that he died so soon after it was published.

Less than two months after Froese's death another underground legend died: Daevid Allen of Gong. In the months prior to his death, Allen instructed the various musicians he was working with to continue recording and touring as Gong. At the time, the band included various musicians, not the least of which was Dave Sturt, formerly of Jade Warrior and Bill Nelson's group. With Allen having announced following his cancer diagnosis that he had months to live, the band played on, Allen enthusiastically supporting them. Gong member Kavus Torabi recalled the situation in a September 2016 interview for *The Guardian*: 'Each night, we sent Daevid recordings or links to YouTube footage, and from his sickbed in Australia, he wrote gushing praise about what had happened to the band and how this was exactly what he had hoped. By the end of the tour, and with the full blessing of Daevid, we decided to carry on'.

I remember being astonished by this revelation, since it seemed to me to be entirely at odds with Gong's founder and beating heart passing away. Yet, as is made clear in the interview, Allen fully supported the move. Why would this be? Well, like so many others, Allen believed in some concept of spirit or soul, and I think that has a lot to do with it. He did not envisage his creation dying with him.

The same situation applied to Edgar Froese. One of the quotes most often mentioned in his obituaries was his comment that, 'There is no death, there is just a change of our cosmic address'.

In his 2009 interview at *Innerviews* with Anil Prasad, Froese elaborated on his personal philosophy:

> I can tell you that I don't believe in death. It's something that's told to people by churches ... Nothing dies, even if it disappears from our visual perception and even if we can't reach it with our other senses. My personal studies – which have been going on for 45 years since the age of fifteen – tell me there is a completely different system and world beyond everything we are experiencing and the system we are jailed in. From here, it goes up. You could call it an elevator.

Froese then had some kind of belief in his essence carrying on after death, and this I think is what he also imagined for his creation Tangerine Dream. As with Gong minus Daevid Allen, I personally find the notion of Tangerine Dream without Froese to be an impossible concept; though many fans have embraced the notion of Thorsten Quaeschning continuing to record and tour under Froese's group name, alongside some of the musicians Froese worked with in his final years.

Thus, Tangerine Dream continued. There was no death of the group; there was just a change of their cosmic address.

On Track series

Tori Amos – Lisa Torem 978-1-78952-142-9

Asia – Peter Braidis 978-1-78952-099-6

Barclay James Harvest – Keith and Monica Domone 978-1-78952-067-5

The Beatles – Andrew Wild 978-1-78952-009-5

The Beatles Solo 1969-1980 – Andrew Wild 978-1-78952-030-9

Blue Oyster Cult – Jacob Holm-Lupo 978-1-78952-007-1

Marc Bolan and T.Rex – Peter Gallagher 978-1-78952-124-5

Kate Bush – Bill Thomas 978-1-78952-097-2

Camel – Hamish Kuzminski 978-1-78952-040-8

Caravan – Andy Boot 978-1-78952-127-6

Cardiacs – Eric Benac 978-1-78952-131-3

Eric Clapton Solo – Andrew Wild 978-1-78952-141-2

The Clash – Nick Assirati 978-1-78952-077-4

Crosby, Stills and Nash – Andrew Wild 978-1-78952-039-2

The Damned – Morgan Brown 978-1-78952-136-8

Deep Purple and Rainbow 1968-79 – Steve Pilkington 978-1-78952-002-6

Dire Straits – Andrew Wild 978-1-78952-044-6

The Doors – Tony Thompson 978-1-78952-137-5

Dream Theater – Jordan Blum 978-1-78952-050-7

Elvis Costello and The Attractions – Georg Purvis 978-1-78952-129-0

Emerson Lake and Palmer – Mike Goode 978-1-78952-000-2

Fairport Convention – Kevan Furbank 978-1-78952-051-4

Peter Gabriel – Graeme Scarfe 978-1-78952-138-2

Genesis – Stuart MacFarlane 978-1-78952-005-7

Gentle Giant – Gary Steel 978-1-78952-058-3

Gong – Kevan Furbank 978-1-78952-082-8

Hawkwind – Duncan Harris 978-1-78952-052-1

Roy Harper – Opher Goodwin 978-1-78952-130-6

Iron Maiden – Steve Pilkington 978-1-78952-061-3

Jefferson Airplane – Richard Butterworth 978-1-78952-143-6

Jethro Tull – Jordan Blum 978-1-78952-016-3

Elton John in the 1970s – Peter Kearns 978-1-78952-034-7

The Incredible String Band – Tim Moon 978-1-78952-107-8
Iron Maiden – Steve Pilkington 978-1-78952-061-3
Judas Priest – John Tucker 978-1-78952-018-7
Kansas – Kevin Cummings 978-1-78952-057-6
Led Zeppelin – Steve Pilkington 978-1-78952-151-1
Level 42 – Matt Philips 978-1-78952-102-3
Aimee Mann – Jez Rowden 978-1-78952-036-1
Joni Mitchell – Peter Kearns 978-1-78952-081-1
The Moody Blues – Geoffrey Feakes 978-1-78952-042-2
Mike Oldfield – Ryan Yard 978-1-78952-060-6
Tom Petty – Richard James 978-1-78952-128-3
Porcupine Tree – Nick Holmes 978-1-78952-144-3
Queen – Andrew Wild 978-1-78952-003-3
Radiohead – William Allen 978-1-78952-149-8
Renaissance – David Detmer 978-1-78952-062-0
The Rolling Stones 1963-80 – Steve Pilkington 978-1-78952-017-0
The Smiths and Morrissey – Tommy Gunnarsson 978-1-78952-140-5
Steely Dan – Jez Rowden 978-1-78952-043-9
Steve Hackett – Geoffrey Feakes 978-1-78952-098-9
Thin Lizzy – Graeme Stroud 978-1-78952-064-4
Toto – Jacob Holm-Lupo 978-1-78952-019-4
U2 – Eoghan Lyng 978-1-78952-078-1
UFO – Richard James 978-1-78952-073-6
The Who – Geoffrey Feakes 978-1-78952-076-7
Roy Wood and the Move – James R Turner 978-1-78952-008-8
Van Der Graaf Generator – Dan Coffey 978-1-78952-031-6
Yes – Stephen Lambe 978-1-78952-001-9
Frank Zappa 1966 to 1979 – Eric Benac 978-1-78952-033-0
10CC – Peter Kearns 978-1-78952-054-5

Decades Series

The Bee Gees in the 1960s – Andrew Mon Hughes et al 978-1-78952-148-1
Alice Cooper in the 1970s – Chris Sutton 978-1-78952-104-7

Curved Air in the 1970s – Laura Shenton 978-1-78952-069-9

Fleetwood Mac in the 1970s – Andrew Wild 978-1-78952-105-4

Focus in the 1970s – Stephen Lambe 978-1-78952-079-8

Genesis in the 1970s – Bill Thomas 978178952-146-7

Marillion in the 1980s – Nathaniel Webb 978-1-78952-065-1

Pink Floyd In The 1970s – Georg Purvis 978-1-78952-072-9

The Sweet in the 1970s – Darren Johnson 978-1-78952-139-9

Uriah Heep in the 1970s – Steve Pilkington 978-1-78952-103-0

Yes in the 1980s – Stephen Lambe with David Watkinson 978-1-78952-125-2

On Screen series

Carry On… – Stephen Lambe 978-1-78952-004-0

David Cronenberg – Patrick Chapman 978-1-78952-071-2

Doctor Who: The David Tennant Years – Jamie Hailstone 978-1-78952-066-8

Monty Python – Steve Pilkington 978-1-78952-047-7

Seinfeld Seasons 1 to 5 – Stephen Lambe 978-1-78952-012-5

Other Books

Babysitting A Band On The Rocks – G.D. Praetorius 978-1-78952-106-1

Derek Taylor: For Your Radioactive Children – Andrew Darlington 978-1-78952-038-5

Iggy and The Stooges On Stage 1967-1974 – Per Nilsen 978-1-78952-101-6

Jon Anderson and the Warriors – the road to Yes – David Watkinson 978-1-78952-059-0

Nu Metal: A Definitive Guide – Matt Karpe 978-1-78952-063-7

Tommy Bolin: In and Out of Deep Purple – Laura Shenton 978-1-78952-070-5

Maximum Darkness – Deke Leonard 978-1-78952-048-4

Maybe I Should've Stayed In Bed – Deke Leonard 978-1-78952-053-8

Psychedelic Rock in 1967 – Kevan Furbank 978-1-78952-155-9

The Twang Dynasty – Deke Leonard 978-1-78952-049-1

and many more to come!

Would you like to write for Sonicbond Publishing?

At Sonicbond Publishing we are always on the look-out for authors, particularly for our two main series:

On Track. Mixing fact with in depth analysis, the On Track series examines the work of a particular musical artist or group. All genres are considered from easy listening and jazz to 60s soul to 90s pop, via rock and metal.

On Screen. This series looks at the world of film and television. Subjects considered include directors, actors and writers, as well as entire television and film series. As with the On Track series, we balance fact with analysis.

While professional writing experience would, of course, be an advantage the most important qualification is to have real enthusiasm and knowledge of your subject. First-time authors are welcomed, but the ability to write well in English is essential.

Sonicbond Publishing has distribution throughout Europe and North America, and all books are also published in E-book form. Authors will be paid a royalty based on sales of their book.

Further details are available from www.sonicbondpublishing.co.uk. To contact us, complete the contact form there or email info@sonicbondpublishing.co.uk